LondonbyLondon
THE INSIDERS' GUIDE 2007

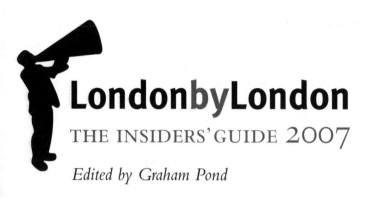

LondonbyLondon

THE INSIDERS' GUIDE 2007

Edited by Graham Pond

FRIDAY BOOKS

First published in Great Britain in 2007 by Friday Books
An imprint of The Friday Project Limited
83 Victoria Street, London SW1H OHW

www.thefridayproject.co.uk
www.fridaybooks.co.uk

British Library Cataloguing in Publication Data

A catalogue record for this book is available
from the British Library

ISBN 13: 978-1-905548-14-9

Design by Staziker Jones
www.stazikerjones.co.uk

Printed by MPG Books Ltd

CONTENTS

WELCOME TO
LONDONBYLONDON

So here we are again: another year, another heart-lifting, rib-tickling, finger-licking slice of concentrated London. Not the fake nonsense 'Laaandon' of TV soap opera and tabloid make-believe, but London as it really is – as it's really lived, loved and loathed by everyday, extraordinary Londoners – Londoners who do the living, loving and loathing firsthand, then write to us to tell us all about it. Within the next 200-plus pages, you will find selected gems from the last year of London by London, the city's best-loved virtual community. This is London without its clothes on, churlish and proud, revelling in all its helpful, hilarious, supportive, sarcastic, beautiful, back-biting glory.

From its humble beginnings in 2002, when a handful of people began sharing their unique and intimate London knowledge via email, to the community of tens of thousands it is today, LbL is gradually establishing itself as the number one resource for intelligent, inquisitive Londoners – as well as those who are merely London-curious. LbL is where people turn if they need to share a touching moment on their daily commute – a song, a conquest, a chatty driver, an out-and-out loon; it's where peeved pedestrians come to get something off their chest before it sends them to A&E; it's where new Londoners with pangs for the past come to track down a lardy cake or some French eggy bread, American-style; and it's where differently-abled Londoners share their past lives and ask questions about limescale and the Queen's purse. And they are never disappointed. Well, rarely.

This year we decided to kick each section off with a couple of words from some of the many Londoners who've been kind enough to take part in our weekly interview over the last year. Not only was this a nice way to ensure that their words were preserved for posterity, but it also meant we could knock off early and not bother writing an introduction of our own.

What follows then is some of the very best that London has to offer – from pie and mash to The London Fox, from tight-fisted celebrities to public loos, from pregnancy and the miracle of birth to grisly, grisly suicide...

All London life is here.

And if you'd like to be a part of the LbL community, pop along to the address below and tell us what you know, ask about what you don't or just pile in and make some friends.

Anon!

www.londonbylondon.co.uk

OBSERVATIONS

LONDON IS... ASBOs FOR PREACHERS and protesters alike; Dan Brown loonies and mashed-up babies, selfish buggers and chuggers that just won't quit; London is awash with the kindness of strangers, random acts of charity and random acts of wrath; London is all the animals under the sun, running free through your bins or, not quite so free, through your digestive tract...

What's the most invigorating thing about London?
'It's a melting pot of cultures. It's still one of the greatest cities in the world for that. And we got some fit women down here.'

 *Noel Clarke,* actor

THE PEOPLE WHO MAKE IT ALL HAPPEN

ASBO PHIL

So the Sinners and Winners man has been given an ASBO. And the Court of Appeal has decided that Brian Haw should be kicked out of Parliament Square. Now, as human beings, I frankly have little time for either of these guys. But neither were doing anyone any harm by their activities, they were simply using their right to free speech. Do we want a London where everyone is the same, where everyone acts the same and thinks the same? Or do we want a London peopled with the odd 'character' who believes in something (even something as patently stupid as Jesus) so strongly that they are willing to put up with ridicule and quite cold weather to make their point? And if we want the latter what can we do now to stand up for Brian and the Sinners and Winners man? As someone famous might say in the future, 'when they came for the Sinners and Winners man I said nothing because I am not a religious nutter with a megaphone; when they came for Brian Haw I said nothing because I don't wear a hat covered in

badges and mumble incomprehensibly; when they came for me there was no one left to speak for me'.

The Assassin Prince

I found out about it when my mate sent me a picture message of him and Phil (the Sinners and Winners man) on Victoria Street. With his lawyer. He asked Phil why he was looking so down and was told that he had got an ASBO. After this had been relayed to me from my mate something very unexpected happened. I felt sad. Something has been taken away from us that made an area of London special. I mean I'm by no means a religious maniac. Far from it. Quite a few sub-vocal curses have been made in his direction as we were assailed by his monotone droning with no escape save the slow trudge into Oxford Circus tube station. But I'm actually going to miss the old bugger. Really wasn't expecting that.

Machine

Absolute balderdash. He followed a friend of mine down the street calling her a sinner, a harlot, and other ancient biblical insults for loose women. Her crime? Wearing a top that showed her arms. A while later he did the same to a friend who was wearing open-toed shoes. In 2001, he said I was going to burn in hell for laying down with other men – all I was doing was walking down the road with two male friends. Good riddance to bad rubbish, and I propose should he ever be seen there again, 400 of us should turn up with megaphones of our own and return the favour. We'll only be exercising our right to free speech, after all. And what's the harm in that?

The man was a disgrace to our city.

Retroboy

I am in the 'good riddance' camp for the Sinners and Winners man. I've worked at Oxford Circus for 5 years and the already stressful, packed streets are a little less stressful now I no longer have his megaphone rattling in my ear on my way to and from work. He had nothing constructive to say and was rude to passers-by. Loudly. Rest assured though – the ASBO hasn't deterred him... just last Saturday he was in Leicester Square. (With megaphone.)

niknaks

I agree with freedom of speech and people being able to say what they like, when they like. But I am pleased that the Sinners and Winners man was taken off the streets of London. As a Christian, I was appalled by his 'you're all going to hell in a handbasket' rantings – quite frankly, if the church want more people to come along and hear the truth about Christianity, a man damning the unfaithful world to hell isn't a great start – the fact that he's known as being 'that mad Bible-basher with a megaphone' is a pretty poor calling card. He once accosted me on the tube and condemned me to hell – when I told him that I was a Christian, he condemned me to hell for not spouting off about my religion and for not alienating the Christian faith by ranting like a madman (well, he didn't put it like that, but you know what I mean). People like this do *nothing at all* to make people want to find out about the church... for goodness sake, *The Da Vinci Code* does more to spur people's intrigue regarding the Christian faith! Good riddance to the madman with the megaphone. Find Christ for yourself.

Rommer

TONY

On the subject of 'London's Best Pubs', best pub to get verbally abused in by a gay one-armed drug-dealer making a complete pain in the arse of himself while he orders drinks and then, when he has received them, says, 'I'll have to go to the cashpoint' – *The Joiner's Arms*, Hackney Road, E2.

bareboy

I too have encountered this one-armed bandit. I heard his arm was amputated after he slept on it for three solid days after a drug OD and lost the feeling in it. Is this possible? Scary. I also once lost to him at a game of pool. How bad must I be?

qaf

Oh my god! I beat the gay one-armed drug-dealer at pool, at the *Fountain* in Tottenham. It was controversial though: we'd been playing two on the black all night, and when I came to play against him (it was winner stays on), I said, 'Free ball, two on the black, no picking up the ball after a foul?' and he nodded. Then he fouled when we were both on the black, I lined it up for my second shot and he went mental saying it was one on the black. Turned into an argument, and in the end I don't think we finished the game. But I won that game, fair and square.

Mestalla

OH

Unfortunately 'One-Arm-Tony' (the swearing, dealing, pool-hustling amputee) who was discussed on this website a few weeks ago sadly died at his home last weekend. The landlord of his favourite

local said of him: 'He may have been a difficult bastard, but he was our difficult bastard.' He truly was an urban legend and the East End salutes the passing of 'one of the greats'. It is great he finally got the recognition he deserved.

 *Junky's Needle Comedy*

LONDON'S WORST

CROWMAN

I was watching TV the other day and suddenly Gary 'the Crowman' Crowley was yelling at me, so I flew into a rage and smashed some precious things. When I had calmed down, I got to wondering if there were any other London celebs who annoy me as much as Crowley. The nearest I could come was Robert Elms... Who are LbLers' least favourite Londoners? Bet you can't beat Crowley.

Bic Reeves

Surely our Beloved Leader – Ken Livingstone. In fact, he's The Anti-Londoner. Witness:

1. The congestion charge, hitting the poorest Londoners the hardest.

2. He doubles the cost of travelling on the tube (despite 'promising' that he wouldn't raise fares at all).

3. Of course, though, none of this bothers Ken – his office managed to spend £4,539 on taxis from April to August 2005 (well, you wouldn't want to get on those dangerous, unreliable and expensive tubes, now would you...?).

4. He gets rid of one of the true icons of London – the Routemaster bus (again, breaking another one of his election 'promises').

5. He's responsible for increases in council tax way above the rate of inflation every single year (partly to pay for his shiny City Hall offices).

6. These tax increases also go towards the £2 million that he spends (every year) on his own personal propaganda news sheet – *The Londoner* (oh the irony!), which seems to exist solely to convince us what a great job he is doing (try actually doing a great job – it might be more effective...).

7. He invites terrorist supporters over for tea and sandwiches – again at tax payers' expense.

Could there be a *worse* Londoner...?

Tim

Jeffrey Archer gets my vote. Him and them troublesome Mitchell brothers.

Josey

LONDON'S BEST

RED KEN

Whilst I agree that Gary Crowley is the scourge of our society, I would much rather accentuate the positive than revel in the negative. So what about London's Best Londoners?! Which Londoners are the greatest ambassadors for this city? Can't think of anyone myself, but would like to hear others' suggestions.

Candice

I'm likely to get myself flamed in the worst way, but I'm willing to suggest Red Ken as one of the Best Londoners. OK, so many of us may whinge about his track record within the past couple of years, but what's undeniable is that he has spent most of the past 30 years campaigning and fighting for a better London, which many LbLers may not realise.

He has lived and worked both North and South (born in Lambeth and served on Camden Council) and has always been on the side of true Londoners. He was instrumental in getting public transport back into mainstream use in the early 1980s when the Tories were all for running it into the ground. He tried national politics for a while, but hated it and returned to what he loves best, London. In years to come, I'm betting that the congestion charge will come to be seen as one of the things that helped to preserve London. I'm not on his pay, nor do I even know Ken (in fact, I've never even met him), but for him to have continued to fight for a cause in which he believes, despite the brickbats that have been thrown at him over the years, deserves a big mention.

Go on – have a moan. I know you will.

robram

Peter Ackroyd and Andrew Duncan both deserve a mention. Ackroyd's novels are fun and full of atmosphere and his 'London' is a great biography of the city. Andrew Duncan's walking books are packed with historical info and snippets of gossip and he's a great guide for our brilliant city.

micky

For single-handedly saving da kids from obesity and heart failure, my vote goes to Jamie Oliver.

Robbie

THE CURSE OF DAN BROWN

well i went to a medeater, who speaks with the dead,
and knows things no one should. i went because i
have spiritual activities in my home. in the
past i had my palms read, and was told of past lives
i've had, sceptical until this woman told me the
same things. they say the holy grail will come to
you. well here i am in human form, but carry the
soul of mary magdalene. i was told i am needed for
end times... i am not crazy, i have a business. i
have spirits more so than any other so i am told that
protect me. i feel energies as well as i have many
orbs on tape in my home. i went to the medium to
find answers to the many things i have seen and
foretold. jesus in the sky, leviathan, and many other
things and had witnesses too. it is not the bones to
be prayed upon, but your lord jesus for he comes
quickly amen. bush is the anti christ. beware.

mary magdalene

hello. i went to a medeater who eats meds and he told
me that i am not a looney and that this is evident by the
way i write i with a small i and not a big i in that i am not
bigging myself up and therefore must not be a looney or
a very small one at the very least. my medeater read my
palms and said they weren't as complex as the *da vinci*

code but the style was much more engaging. i will scan them later and put them on the internet for everyone to read. i have a scanner because i have a business, further proof that i must not really be a looney but actually someone very important hiding in someone else and in a good way too and not like a bad person waiting to say boo. laters.

Pokeyozo

See? Reading *The Da Vinci Code* is bad for your health!

AdamM

LONDON'S SCARIEST...

PSYCHO

I wish to share my disturbing experience on my commute to work by bicycle this morning in a bid for therapeutic cleansing. On cycling through Clissold Park a child of about seven came haring towards me, also on a bicycle, and at the last second before impact skidded away and laughed. Somewhat shocked and surprised, I turned to look at the fast retreating child, shook my head and said 'bloody hell' – not loudly, i.e. the child couldn't hear me,

however on turning round I saw that his approaching father (about 60ish, also on bike) did. As I cycled past him he turned his bike round and came after me, screaming his head off. I kept cycling, more than a little worried and he screamed that I'd better not keep on cos he'd catch me and 'fucking do me in'.

Not quite sure what to do and panicked, I paused and turned to face him, when I was faced with a volley of screamed abuse that I shouldn't look at his kid like that (and I mean screamed and with a volley of insults, swearing – that his kid could certainly hear – and threats of death if he ever saw me again). I tried to cycle away again and he came after me again, overtook me, spun to a halt, threw his bike on the ground and started up again with the screaming from about two inches away from my face. Which, incidentally, was when I noticed the teardrop tattooed under his eye. (I recalled immediately that this is a prison tattoo signifying something nasty.)

I was petrified and shocked at this point and asked him (with lots of effort, calmly) to leave me alone and told him that his shouting was scaring me. To which he screamed that 'oh yes, you should be scared, cos he'd...' at which point a family rounded the corner looking extremely worried and perturbed by the noise. I took the opportunity to take off at speed and he continued to chase me shouting until I managed to cross Green Lanes by jumping the red light and whizzing through a gap in the stream of traffic which finally halted him (leaving his kids somewhere alone in the park). I wasn't sure he'd stopped and, adrenaline pumping, I cycled a convoluted high speed route taking lots of rights and lefts all the way to Soho.

Yes, I shouldn't have said 'bloody hell' to a retreating child but it was an exclamation of surprise and not quite reason for this volley of scary abuse and being chased through the park in a hugely threatening way (I am, by the way, a petite 5′2″ female). I really think if the family had not shown up he would have hit me he seemed so worked up. I am now scared to cycle through the park tonight or ever again in case he goes there regularly and sees me again (he seemed the type to bear a grudge). So, a warning to anyone else who sees a man with prison tatts in Clissold to avoid him at all costs. Has anyone else had a run in with him? (And lived to tell the tale...?) How could I have handled this better? Where can I buy mace???

 milkandtwo

Easy for me to say, but don't you dare stop using the park – just maybe not when it's dark. You've as much right to use it as Psycho and his son (to whom he is obviously setting a fine example) and if you stop, then he would undoubtedly see it as a moral victory. When you next cycle through the park, just take it nice and calmly and watch where you're going. Chances are, if he sees you he won't remember a thing about the contretemps as he was probably high on something and/or has the intellectual capacity of a walnut and thus doesn't remember anything he did five minutes ago. If he does threaten you verbally, go straight to the police – from what you say, they'll know him well anyway and you don't have to press charges – they'll give you some sympathetic advice if nothing else. Good luck.

HamptonCaught

Deeply disturbed by this story. I live in Newington Green and am aware of said psycho. I wouldn't describe him as a friend, but he can lose his rag from time to time. Unfulfilled life and a little frustrated and sad. Will have a word – please continue to cycle, and put this behind you.

Man-like-Beth

THIEF

A couple of weeks ago I saw three kids try to snatch a handbag from a woman on the London Bridge to Dartford train while it was stopped at Deptford. She was sitting near the door and they jumped on and tried to grab it. Fortunately, she managed to hang on to it and they ran off with nothing. However, a bit of a reminder not to leave your bag on the seat next to you, especially if you're sitting near the doors. As an aside, several people sitting nearby checked that she was OK, congratulated her for hanging on and started a bit of a chat. Turns out it's not the first time that it's happened to her on that train line, so beware!

C Fi

Is it legal to punch people (kids, adults, whatever) who try to grab things like this? *Please* say it is!

Zabadak

I believe the law lets you use reasonable force. Still if I saw you punch someone trying to steal your bag, I wouldn't admit to seeing it.

Stiltskin

Stop thief!

Bag theft. Everyone knows someone that this has happened to. Did you know the police don't separate out this type of crime in their public reports? I think it's a very under-reported crime that happens countless times every night in London alone. I have a new website www.bagtheftblog.com that attempts to record instances of handbag theft and maps them. It will hopefully build up a picture across London and the rest of the country of where it happens and how often, and help people avoid it happening to them. To report a crime there's a form to email me on the map page, or email me at report@bagtheftblog.com. A quick email with details of date, place, and so on, would be of great interest. Please pass on to your friends, family, male or female, anyone and everyone who might know someone who's been affected by this! Together we can make things better. Thanks for your help!

Bag Theft

LONDON'S MOST IRRITATING...

CHUGGERS

I am now going to have to officially call time on chuggers. They are becoming increasingly rude and belligerent (especially those on Oxford Street) and unless their respective charities don't call them back in, I'm going to hurt one of them. As an example, one tried to collar me the other day and already having dealt with several of his colleagues, I ignored him (as is my right). He carried on shouting after me, eventually bawling 'Oi!' at the top of his voice. I continued to ignore him, because if I had turned round, I would have stuck my foot so far up his arse that he'd have tasted shoe polish. I don't give a shit about the worthiness of their causes. If I want to donate, I'm not going to give my money to some brass-necked gobshite on a percentage. I think you should join me in writing to any charity you see soliciting funds in this way and suggest that they fucking stop it.

Stevie Bee

The walk down Neal Street has become perilous due to chuggers. I had to explain to one that when they see me coming and stand in my path and I move to the other side of the street, that is me actively avoiding them and not inviting them to also move across the street and wave their arms in my face. I had to call a charity the other day and report the aggressive and abuse behaviour/language used on me by one I ignored...

Sibslock

Get a pram. Chuggers completely ignore me now when I'm out and about with my baby boy. They just look past me toward their next possible target. I wonder why?

PopC

One tactic I've started using against these guilt-inducing little feckers is to tell them straight up that you think their cause is indeed a very worthy cause, but if they manage to convince you to donate to their charity, then you will do it directly through the charity so they get the full amount of your donation, and the chugger receives nowt. Then offer the chugger the choice to either carry on talking if they actually care about the charity, or if they're just in it for the cut, to move on to somebody else. Twice I've used that, and the look on their faces as they struggle to think of a suitable answer (before saying 'forget it') is priceless. It's great to turn the guilt back on them for a change!

Gizzard

Saying 'No thank you' also works.

Petal

Why Petal, what a fantastic tip. The simple methods are always the best, eh? I assume that since this works for you, you helpfully decided to let us other, far more pointlessly elaborate people know about your quick 'n' easy avoidance method? Next time you decide to take the effort of writing to LbL with your simple tips, please keep in mind that your own experiences with chuggers do not necessarily reflect everyone else's, and in fact if it was a simple case of saying 'no thank you', then people wouldn't feel the need to write in to LbL about them in the first place, or create websites such as this: www.bloodychuggers.co.uk, would they?

Gizzard

Classic LbL. A pointless rant, a lovely little putdown and then another, bruised pride inspired, pointless rant. I love it. Keep it coming people...

cdouble

SELFISH BUGGERS

Over the past few weeks, we have had subjects discussing buying tickets (or not) for the underground and buses, parking scooters (legally or not), opening bus doors with the emergency buttons (fineable or not) and not to forget the bikes not stopping at red lights (stupid or not)! I have to say that I am getting a bit worried about the state of the town. Surely, people must understand that there are rules in place to ensure safety and order of the person and society as a whole… Why is it that we who love London do our utmost to rebel against it and its rules? What makes us so single-minded and selfish as to say, 'I can't wait, I do not agree or I'm not included in this rule, therefore it's my right to ignore or to bend it?'

 ThePnut

Beautifully put. People just don't understand (or appreciate) quite how good they have it with life in London and this country in general. There's a lot of talk about civil liberties and freedom in the media at the moment. What a lot of people fail to recognise is that freedom comes at a price. Fifty years ago it was the lives of thousands of people. Today it is simply what is known as a 'duty of care' to your fellow citizens (bus drivers included) and respecting very simple laws and rules. If you don't like the rules here, move somewhere else. Try Zimbabwe or Afghanistan.

Notmyfault

Londonders selfish? Possibly – however, you can't blame us. It can't be just me that feels it's take, take, take from the powers that be in this city. I'm reminded of Tony Blair's drive for respect. The day a Southern Trains employee, traffic warden, tube worker, council worker or dare I mention Ken shows me respect then I'll know something's working. And if that sounds like a rant it is – partly because I was 20 minutes late for work this morning *again* because nobody cares enough to manage Victoria station effectively.

Nice Londoner

I like Londoners – beats where I come from – shops are closed on Wednesday afternoons and trying to get a pint of milk is like a trek into the wilderness (last time it took me nearly three hours!). And you can forget takeaway pizzas! Living in close proximity to lots of people means we need to be tolerant – small price to pay for the wonderful experience of meeting such a diverse lot of neighbours...

JP

Mash up

My dad was driving through Brixton when, a bit fast, he came speeding round the corner and went into the back of this guy's car stopped at some lights. Nothing dramatic, just a bit of a shunt. No visible marks though. The guy gets out the car, already angry. 'You mash up me car!' he shouts. My dad just stands there not knowing what to say as a crowd of people begin to gather. The guy says 'You mash up me car!' a couple more times then he goes back into the car, picks up a baby and he comes back out. 'You mash up me car and you mash up me baby!' As the crowd of people start passing this development around – 'he said he mash up his car and he mash up his baby' – my dad asks the guy if he can offer him some financial recompense and the guy says, 'Yeah, give me a tenner'. And that was that. Gotta love Brixton.

John C

THE KINDNESS OF STRANGERS

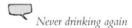

THANKS

Just wanted to say thanks to the lovely person who asked me what was wrong when I was walking aimlessly near Old Street on Easter Thursday night crying due to drinking way too much alcohol and getting upset over something rather small in hindsight, but rather traumatic at the time. That was very nice of you and you made me feel a whole lot better to know that someone cared. Everyone else kind of looked at me and must have thought I was a psycho... not that I was really in any state to notice or care, mind you. I really was in a bit of state. So thanks.

Has anyone else been helped by a stranger?

Never drinking again

I was living on my own in Fulham a couple of years ago, and on arriving home after a Christmas party discovered I no longer had any house keys. My new 'spare set' being locked in the flat, I didn't really know what to do. I was trying to figure out where to go, and was on the verge of tears myself, when some girls stopped and asked if I was

OK. I explained said conundrum, and they invited me into their flat for a party. They also let me sleep on their sofa, and I have never been more grateful. In hindsight this could have been horrendously dangerous...

drankinor pissedagain

Not shouting 'cunt', mugging or ripping me off... just leaning across with an umbrella and, walking beside me, sharing his personal space to keep me dry till I got to my bus stop in Colliers Wood. Great moment – and no I'm not blonde, leggy or actually female. Well done that man! And thank you.

Dry Londoner

I was in a similar state just a year ago, had just had my phone and wallet nicked, and a very nice crack-whore showed me his underground car park (to escape the torrential rain), gave me his tobacco, papers, lighter and a pound to get home on the night bus. Who says Londoners are unfriendly?

burgeoned alcoholic

I've sat next to you on the 133 to Streatham. Nice hat.

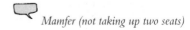
Mamfer (not taking up two seats)

DHL?! You must be mental

I WANT YOU TO HELP TO LONDON SO THAT WE CAN BE TO CONTACT IN WHATEVER MEANS BECAUSE I DONT HAVE ANY HOPE EXCEPT YOU PLEASE MAY GOD BLESS YOU. PLZ SEND TO ME EITHER BY INVITATION LETTER OR ANY MEANS THANKS. I'M IN HASTE TO GET IN TOUCH WITH YOU, I WANT TO WITNESS SEEING YOU OVER THERE, PLZ IF YOU WANT TO SEND ME THE INVITATION LETTER SEND ME THROUGH DHL SO THAT IT WILL BE FAST, I PRAY THAT GOD WILL CONTINUE TO BLESS YOU IN JESUS NAME AMEN. LONDON BY LONDON WILL NEVER COLLAPSE IN JESUS NAME AMEN.

WALEX

Sights and sounds

POETRY

I would just like to share my small sadness at the loss of one piece of London that always engaged me: the large blue words 'I LOVED YOU' daubed forlornly across the edge of the roof of a house on Pembridge Road, W11. I don't know why it was painted but speculated endlessly. What could drive someone to go to the trouble? A dig at a callous ex over the road? A parting paean to the pub there before the Prince Albert's modern stylings moved in? Or was it painted first without the D as a true expression of love, only deep nagging pessimism making the writer leave room for that all important letter? I'll never know, and it will now slide gradually from my memory. Unless, of course, the current owner of the place feels as I do that that corner of London is better off knowing of his/her erstwhile love, and repaints it afresh onto the soon-to-be-shiny new frontage. I can only hope.

Eltanin

LOUD LONDON

If we're having a moan about non-thinking wankers on public transport, can I nominate people who listen to their portable music devices so loud that I can identify not only the song and the singer, but also detect the studio sound engineer's slight asthma problem? My concern isn't that these people will be damaging their hearing with every passing decibel, but rather that it makes it really difficult to concentrate with an incessant tssssska-tssssska-tssssska in the vicinity. I reckon that if I can hear the music from your headphones louder than whatever's coming through mine, then it's too loud. And if I can't read or think blankly, or listen to music or the radio when I'm commuting, then I shall go slightly mad. In the meantime, my solution is to (with great subtlety, natch) mouth the words of the song they are listening to, in time to the music, and try to catch their eye. It tends to freak them out a little. Any other solutions?

Louden Kleah

In response to Louden Kleah and his moan about people listening to personal stereos. I myself do not leave the house without my trusty iPod. I do this for the following reasons. (a) The tube is a dismal, joyless, cramped, mundane and all-round nasty experience for such an early time of the day. Listening to my favourite music on the way to another hard day in the office gets me through the journey a little happier. (b) It drowns out the sound of the annoying tube drivers who have a remarkable knack of telling you absolutely nothing of use when you need it, but who insist on telling you the same piece of crap information over and over again... 'this train is for Aldgate, all stations to Aldgate, calling at all stations, terminating at Aldgate. this is an Aldgate train'. Thanks. I only get it every day. On top of this there is of course (c) the sound of the train, the doors closing and opening, the occasional conversation between other people, mobile phones, and a multitude of other sounds. Other people's stereos then is one of many sounds that one may endure on the way to a destination.

If you want peace and tranquillity in order to concentrate, might I suggest one of the many libraries or museums. If neither of these are suitable for transporting you to work, a cab! Failing that, if noise offends you so much, you could try ear plugs, a personal stereo of your own, or moving, to perhaps somewhere which isn't the most noisy city in the entire country. *Or* you could do what everyone else does, read your *Metro*, get on with it, find some way of making the experience a little more enjoyable and relax, safe in the knowledge that you will probably be there in about ten minutes' time.

Ipodder

I'd like to thank Ipodder for missing the point of my original post in such a lengthy and thorough way. If you re-read my original comment, you'll notice that I wasn't actually moaning about people listening to personal stereos – on the contrary, I even referred to my own personal listening habits – but rather about the anti-social volume at which some people do so. While I appreciate that the sound of doors closing and opening must be extremely distracting, do you really need to have the volume up so loud that I can hear your music even through the barriers presented by your earphones, the air and general hubbub of transport, my earphones and my music? My dear, if your music is louder than mine in my ears, then it's too loud and you shall damage your hearing. Or miss an important announcement. Or have someone attack your headphones with nail scissors. Or all of the above.

While ALRIGHT ALRIGHT ALRIGHT OK NOW LADIES, I'm writing (YEAH!), let me just say WE GON' BREAK THIS THING DOWN how IN JUS' A FEW SECONDS happy DON'T HAVE ME BREAK THIS THANG DOWN FOR NOTHIN' I am that I WANNA SEE Y'ALL ON YO' BADDEST BEHAVIOUR you enjoy music, LEND ME SOME SUGA', I AM YO' NEIGHBOUR, and AHHHH HERE WE GO that you have found a good SHAKE IT! SHAKE IT! SHAKE IT! SHAKE IT! OH OHH! way to SHAKE IT! SHAKE IT! SHAKE IT! SHAKE

IT! make your journey SHAKE IT! SHAKE IT LIKE A POLAROID PICTURE! SHAKE IT! SHAKE IT! less dull. Good SHH YOU GOT TO SHAKE IT! for SHHH SHAKE IT! you. See how annoying it is?

However if, as you seem to suggest, you turn the volume up in order to drown out other people's anti-socially loud in-ear music, then I must conclude that the whole world is going to hell in a selfish handbasket, because two wrongs do not, and never have, made a right.

Also, I'm a girl. Not that it makes any difference whatsoever.

Louden Kleah (Mrs)

MOBILE MUSIC

As annoying as people listening to their iPods too loud are, there's an even worse culprit on public transport (particularly buses). Stupid people who play music from their mobile phones without headphones so that the *entire* bus, carriage, street or store has to listen to their crappy taste in music. These phones have awful speakers so the sound is all staticky and terrible, and usually they insist on playing the worst form of R&B and hip-hop available. Maybe if I heard someone playing a decent

song I would feel differently… but that's never been an issue. For some reason it's usually packs of skiving adolescents annoying me on the 55 bus into town.

Hackney Texan

Is that what that noise was? I thought someone just had their stereo turned up *really* loud! Feel stupid now. I have to confess, sometimes I do turn my iPod up to full volume on the train, but it's only to drown out the sound of some idiot who thinks the rest of us want to listen to their telephone conversation. When they stop I'll happily turn it back down again. Unfortunately I can't usually hear when they hang up! Do feel free to ask me to turn it down again, though. I'm never offended but I reserve the right to politely tell you to fuck off if it's your conversation I was trying not to hear in the first place.

Shutting up now.

always delayed

Conductor

In the 'other people's annoying music' vein, I was on the bus the other day listening to the Grieg piano concerto, which has an ending I just have to conduct. Anyway, I was getting very much into it as I reached the end of the last movement, even adding a little foot movement on the last chord, when I looked up, to find about five people grinning at me! I hope this was more amusing than annoying.

H of Brockers

Has anyone else seen the guy me and my friends call The Conductor? I've seen him a few times now on the bus, conducting to what sounds like the Grieg piano concerto (his music device is invariably on full volume). On a good day he may even add a little foot movement for your amusement.

stylish kid in the riot

SCREECH

Has anyone else heard an excruciating high-pitched noise in and around Liverpool Street station? I had always assumed that it was something to do with the departure screens in the station, but the other day I was in a pub near the station, and it was even louder there! It's a high-pitched whine, similar to that which you get from television screens or computer monitors, but with a pulse to it. Since it is so very high-pitched, your hearing has to be set quite high to hear it, meaning that most men and older women will not be able to, but I'm sure some of you younger, female LbLers must be aware of it...?!

H of Brockers

Yes, I hear it too! I have only met one other person who has heard it as well and he's legally blind (I'm a 30-year-old woman, by the way). It's a horrible throbbing high-pitched thing that makes me feel vaguely nauseous. Neither my blind friend nor I could get to the bottom of it, though. Maybe it's some animal repellent? I've only noticed it there the last couple of years, so something has changed recently...

Monkeys Ahoy!

Sounds very much like the Mosquito – are you under 20 perchance? It's used as a teenager deterrent – perhaps the pub is using it? Would be nice to have areas where they are used publicised. Anybody know if this info is available?

roti&doubles

ELMS DISEASE

Following on from the discussion about iPods. Is anyone else really irritated by the Robert Elms booming message in the lift that they play which drowns out my music. Why does it have to be so loud? I find it even more irritating that he gets email alerts half way through the recording. Listening to my iPod on the way to work is my only quiet time in the day to escape from the incessant emails and phone calls I get all day. Now I have to hear it on the way in as well. Does it actually help tourists? No.

Pointless

After weeks of having to listen to Robert Elms in the lifts at Covent Garden tube station every morning, listening out for the Outlook email alert halfway through, who else was shocked into consciousness after a mind-numbing tube ride this week when, instead of

Robert's dulcet tones, Johnny Vaughan blasted through the speakers??? Nothing quite like it to inspire tube rage...

chocogrl

I do love LbL but sometimes I wish you'd be a little less negative. I've been in that lift with Robert Elms chatting away a few times before and barely noticed it, but after reading that post I felt slightly enraged myself when I next heard it. Obviously my own fault for being so susceptible to comments. God help me if a hypnotist ever gets hold of me.

FabSal

Shrine

I live in Brixton and have always puzzled about something, but am sure someone must know my answer. On the side of the Ritzy which is on Coldharbour Lane there is a small colourful shrine thing in the wall. Has anyone else seen it? Does anyone know why it is there?

Bablet

I've always loved that – the fact that someone carefully cut up pieces of glitzy wrapping paper to fit each individual brick. No real idea who did it but it was put up there around 2000 when I worked there. Suspicion fell on a man who used to come in just as we opened, barge past all the ushers and race into one of the cinemas to sit and smoke B&H fags. Or it could have been the man I had to throw out for having a wank in screen 5... Aah, independent cinemas.

lala

OBJETS D'ERRANT

UNPLEASANT SMELL

Has anyone noticed the pheasant slowly decaying in Waterloo station platform 10 by the buffer stops? Does anyone know what needs doing to remove it as the station staff won't touch it? And while we are on the subject, do we know of any other strange items in places they shouldn't be? There is a pram on a bus shelter in Clapham High Street!

Robin Hood

I've seen a bowl of cornflakes with a nicely posed carton of milk next to it on top of a bus shelter – somewhere on the 243 bus route I think.

The Routemaster

On the subject of 'strange items in places they shouldn't be', I have several to add to Robin Hood's list, which I had the fortune (misfortune?) to observe on my daily number 68 bus route in the spring of last year. Here is the definitive list of what I spied from the top deck looking down onto the top of bus shelters...

Elephant and Castle bus shelter: a crab (and a pretty big one at that – dead, obviously)

Denmark Hill bus shelter: a toilet brush accompanied by a plunger (a nice double act I thought)

Camberwell Green bus shelter: a frying pan (with no lid) with a half-cooked egg in it

Was this just some art student 'aving a larf?

Petroleum Jelly

LOCUST

Does anyone know what the large, gold locusts on Lombard Street and on the *Royal Exchange* in the City symbolise? Have asked everyone I know but can't get a answer.

Insect

The locust is the sign of John the Baptist (the Gospels say he ate locust) and, before it was destroyed in the Great Fire of London, there was a *St John the Baptist Church* on Walbrook, London EC4. I couldn't be 100% certain, but I'm guessing that the proximity of the former church to the buildings you mention is the reason for this.

robram

They symbolise the banks and financial corporations which have infested the area, sucking the humanity, soul and life of those who deign to pass though.

Fi

This is not a locust but a grasshopper, the family emblem of Thomas Gresham, the founder of *The Royal Exchange*. There are golden grasshoppers adorning the weathervanes on the roof and stone grasshoppers carved into the outer walls of the building. The story I've been told is that when Thomas Gresham was lost as a baby in a field of grass, he was found by a child chasing a grasshopper. The grasshopper still appears on the Gresham family crest. If you want to know more then go on any walk guided by Graham at www.walks.com. He is full of knowledge of things like this and a fantastically entertaining guide. Don't forget to ask him about the ghostly fingerprint at the *George and Vulture* restaurant!

Sharky The Shark Dog

Letters
As I was trundling up through Kennington this morning in the direction of The Temple of Mithras, I was struck by a thought. What do those discs on top of

bus stops that have initials on them represent? Is it some sort of mad London quiz – 'collect the letters and make a word!' – or do they have a purpose?

Mamfer (top deck)

Hey Mamfer, you're right, you've discovered the secret underground game, London Omnibus Letters, or LOL for short. I'm currently only an HY away from 'ichthyology' which should at last take me up to Journeyman level. Anyway, as I mentioned it's a secret underground game, so only the initiated know about it, but clearly people started asking questions about these weird red discs everywhere. A cover story had to be contrived, so the Grand Master came up with the amazing idea of pretending that the letters were place markers on local bus maps, allowing the peons to find their correct stop at busy, multi-stop interchanges like Oxford Circus or Trafalgar Square. Oh how I've chuckled to myself watching people consult these imaginary charts! Haha!

uberrich

NO A.M... NO CRY

NO I DONT WANT A COPY OF FUCKING CITY A.M. STOP WAVING IT IN MY FACE AND GET THE FUCK OUT OF MY WAY.

fishface

I found an effective way of dealing with them is to react like the paper is made of toxic waste. Looking horrified with a loud 'Urrrrghhh' is good or take the paper and scream '*It burns, it burns!*' and throw it on the floor. At least the five or so people behind you will then make it through unmolested.

amazon

I agree wholeheartedly with the anti-*City A.M.* sentiment but disagree that it's a cheap version of the *FT*. The *FT* is a well-resourced paper that does attempt to give its readers balanced national and international news (I don't work for them but as a do-gooder press officer I reckon it's the fairest of the lot). *City A.M.* is a loutish pile of junk that thinks that everyone who works in the city is a cigar-chomping wide boy from Essex, high-rolling around on a massive pay packet. Obviously the truth is less 'American Psycho' and much more thousands of bored, unfulfilled people trudging to their long, unsatisfying and not always well-paid jobs. Boycott the rag.

Dave

Hey!!!! I WORK THERE...! It's a FINANCIAL and BUSINESS paper, not a general newspaper. As for being a cheap *FT*... I guess yes, but check the latest readership figures and according to INDEPENDENT surveys we're dumping on the opposition from quite a height (smug mode). I myself barely read a word of it – I couldn't give a monkey's about business and finance. In summary, unless you are a business type, it's not really aimed at you (despite what the poor sods in blue might be persuading you to think with their newspaper waving). I mean, does the average Joe buy the *FT* when there's all the others available? No. And having been in the newspaper business a few years now, it's a damn sight better than many rags I've encountered. Further questions or comments regarding the news business will be gladly fielded.

Snapper

Snapper, I have a question about the news business... do you OFTEN file copy in CAPS to make it MORE NEWSY?

OR NOT?

ils

ALL ROADS LEAD TO...WHERE EXACTLY?

LONDON TOWN

Motorway signage which tells you how far you are from London – what point does it measure from? Is it the tip of Eros' arrow in Piccadilly Circus? I would like to think so.

Karaoke Girl

Motorway stats for mileage to London are based on the distance to the post office in the centre-most part of London.

eyehatelondon

I have recently been told that it is Hyde Park Corner, and that the address of the large building on the north side (1, London) testifies to this. Previously, I had believed the measuring point to be Charing Cross. I have to say I'm not entirely sure which is right, but I reckon that someone else will.

Declan

As far as I know Eros doesn't actually have an arrow, the dude is shooting blanks... but to answer your question: the statue of Charles I on horseback in Trafalgar Square is the official centre of London. I was told that by one of the London tour bus guides and don't just take his word for it either, here's a comment from indieLondon – 'if, like me, you've ever wondered from what point all "distances from London" are measured, *Charles I* marks the spot'.

gazsux

I'm afraid I must dash Karaoke Girl's fantasies. The centre of London is officially measured from the area including Trafalgar Square and Charing Cross. It was officially recognised in 1955, although was backed up centuries earlier by the venerable Samuel Johnson when he wrote of the area: 'the full tide of human existence is here'.

robram

There's a plaque on the ground just south of Trafalgar Square where all distances are measured from. The plaque marks the spot where once stood one of the original 12 crosses commissioned by Edward I to mark the death of Queen Eleanor.

iSleepDiagonal

In general, distances from London (e.g. it's 982 miles
from London to Paris) are measured from the
monument in the yard outside Charing Cross station.
But motorway distances are, confusingly, measured to
the exit you will have to take.

Gonad the Violator

By the way, it's not Eros, it's the Angel of Christian
Charity.

Mamfer

It's not Eros and not the Angel of Christian Charity. It's
intended to be Anteros, a brother of Eros, and is
recorded as such in the records of Westminster City
Council. The sculptor Alfred Gilbert had already
sculpted a statue of Anteros, when commissioned for the
Shaftesbury Memorial Fountain, and chose to reproduce
the same subject, who as 'the God of Selfless Love' was
deemed to suitably represent the philanthropic seventh
Earl of Shaftesbury. Gilbert described Anteros as
portraying 'reflective and mature love, as opposed to
Eros or Cupid, the frivolous tyrant'. The model for the
sculpture was a 16-year-old Italian, whose name appears
to have vanished from history. The fountain, when
originally placed, was meant to have Anteros pointing
his bow towards Wimborne Saint Giles in Dorset, which
was the Earl's country-seat. So no arrow either.

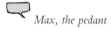

Max, the pedant

WILDLIFE

FISH

So, is it better to throw your apple core (or other biodegradable food waste) into the Thames (for the fish, seagulls etc.) or should I keep it until I find a bin (contributing to landfill)? I walk over Blackfriars Bridge every day and want to know what people think is best.

FireIce

Whilst snorkelling in Thailand I was told by the boat driver (this guy was no captain) that fish loved to snack on pineapple, melon rinds and other such things that his passengers liked to throw into the water, but they were unable to digest the food and it slowly killed them. Shortly after this one of the crew tipped a load of melon rinds and pineapple into the water to please the crowd on the boat. I don't know who to believe so I'd put apple cores in the bin to be on the safe side.

smashedhat

Fish don't like apple. At least the ones in the *Japanese Garden* in Holland Park don't (very beautiful spot by the way). One summer's day some kids were trying to feed them with stones (they were very young) so when they went I thought I'd treat them with some real food instead and was pleased to see the massive Koi bobbing up to gobbled up bits of my yummy braeburn. Only once I'd dropped in just about all of it did they start spitting it out! All of it! A carpet of apple bits on the pond! What a waste of a jolly nice bit of fruit. So you see, fish don't like apple.

FabSal

I think you should let it be eaten by the London wildlife and do the world good. When I have left-over food, that's what I do. Although not being a litterer, I always feel guilty and think people must think I am littering randomly and disrespectfully.

Nerys

Nerys. Are you simple? The only 'wildlife' in London are rats, pigeons and foxes, all of which spread disease. If you want to dump old food waste, do it in your garden and see how long it is before you wake up in the morning with your house filled with unwanted guests.

exterminate

RATS

My mate does pest control for Lambeth. He told me that rats live only where people live. You are never more than ten feet away from a rat in central London. He also told me that a third of the world's food supply is consumed or destroyed by rats. London is full of the nasty, horrible, evil little blighters. My mate also reckons that when he squashes rats, their eyes pop out. Good.

Miss Moneypenny

The reason that we are surrounded by rats is that we, as a race, are a wasteful blight on our surroundings, and think it is acceptable to throw our rubbish every which way we like. The rats are just exploiting our hatred for the world around us. Rather than kill rats, kill the wankers who fly-tip or let their bins flood over, or simply those who can't be bothered to use a dustbin in the first place. I expect their eyes pop when squashed as well. Rats are lovely – they aren't evil. They are only dirty because we create a dirty environment for them. We are the filthy buggers. Not them!

Mad King Soup

I don't recall the great plague starting because some careless wainwright fly-tipped his bag of rat parasites in

Dalston. Rats can eat virtually anything, and thrive in even the cleanest cities. Furthermore, some sources state that rats and other rodent pests consume or destroy anything up to one-third of the world's food supply. As for whether they are good or evil – I somehow doubt a rat can understand concepts more refined than 'pleasure', 'pain', 'hunger' and 'hot ratty fucking'. You can't apply good or evil to an automaton, even if it is fluffy.

Drumbo

THE LONDON FOX

I'm an Australian and recently moved to central London. Yesterday I saw a fox on the balcony of my flat. I couldn't believe my eyes! Anyone else seen it?

Aussie gal

The London Fox? Yeah I've seen him – fox-coloured with foxy ears and a nose like a fox? Yeah, I see him quite a bit. You must live near me.

bushbabyfish

Hi Aussie gal – and welcome to one of the wonders of central London – the skyborn foxes. Some animals adapt to live anywhere and the urban fox has been on the city scene for a long time, but about a decade ago – I guess in response to high-rise developments – they became 'skyborn'. It's unexpected and rather like the huge flocks of parrots you see in parts of south and west London, which are supposed to be the descendants of Jimmy Hendrix's escaped pet – no, really! All true. Anyway, the last I heard there were over 80 breeding couples of skyborn foxes around central and west London.

knowitall

Ah, so you're from Australia. Do you know James?

SFULG

Wow, Aussie Gal! That is *amazing!* I was walking down Oxford Street the other day and I saw a bloke looking *really* bored holding a sign saying 'Golf Sale'! I couldn't believe my eyes! Has anyone else seen him?

Miss Moneypenny

There are loads of foxes in central London. I have seen many in the Borough and London Bridge areas. But I also hear them at night (is that a baby being tortured in Abney Park Cemetery? No, it's the local foxes, getting it on.). I would love to know where they actually live. Is anyone aware of fox dens in London?

ronnie

THEY SHOOT FOXES, DON'T THEY?

We've got a fox den in our back garden. A year ago it was cute, meaning our garden was the playground for seven gambolling fox cubs (awwwwwww). Now it's full of mangy, flea-bitten, occasionally dying foxes – totally unlike the BBC wildlife film I was expecting. I had the RSPCA round once to try and catch a particularly unhealthy specimen that insisted on dying unpleasantly in front of the patio doors – and they said that the urban fox has a very tough life. The fox didn't die, but ran away on what were definitely its last legs. Our garden is now like a public convenience for foxes. The final straw came when they started bringing back used nappies on bin day. I now hate them. If you had to clean up after them, so would you.

Ad

I'm not sure if this is true, but you could try peeing in and around the den. It has to be male urine, as the testosterone content intimidates the males. If you use female urine, your garden might become known among the fox community as the local meeting place (would it be known as 'foxing' – dogging for foxes? I digress...) Anyway, it could bear some further research, or even a trial run. Just get some mates around, supply them with beer and rugby or football and then let 'em at it! But don't forget the door mat!

The Envoy

There is a small chance I will make myself unpopular here, but here goes... Ad, I feel sorry for you and want to help. The vermin problem that you are having is a trying one and jolly well done you for involving the RSPCA. There are a couple of solutions to your problem that I present for your consideration, but first, as a general enquiry, you should phone the Council and find out how they deal with foxes on municipal land as this may help you decide a course of action.

My first suggestion is that you dig the foxes out, i.e. totally destroy their home and they will then probably go elsewhere. The nature of your garden may rule this out, and in doing this there is the possibility of coming face to face with a slightly pissed-off fox... Bear in mind that from the moment you corner any animal, it becomes captive in the eyes of the law and you must not (and should not wish to) harm it at all. Poison is not an option because of the risk of killing some hapless creature that should not be killed (someone's pet for example).

So, my second and favoured suggestion is that you solve the problem cheaply and efficiently by the judicious and careful use of an air rifle. Air rifles can be bought legally if you are over 17 years old and the rifle falls within the legal limit for power (12lb/ft^2). Feral foxes are classed as vermin, just like the horrible pigeon or the lovely magpie (because it eats other birds' eggs). All of these vermin can be killed with impunity. As long as you confine this bloodthirsty activity strictly to the bounds of your garden, and you are humane, then happy days, as they say. The only problem you may have is if a neighbour sees the rifle they may get the wrong idea and call the five-oh, but in this instance, when you wipe off the face paint and explain yourself reasonably all will be well.

I cannot stress enough, be very careful not to scare your neighbours. Perhaps let them know what you are doing. Get the most powerful .22 air rifle you are legally able to (foxes are tough and will need finishing-off, so to speak, if you take one down without taking it out) and practise with it until you are better than the Jackal and James Bond put together. Develop ice-cold nerves and a cool steely Man With No Name stare. Call your house 'Deadwood' or 'Sleepy Hollow' or similar and then ruthlessly begin dealing swift death to the foxes. No mercy is your mantra. Local cat owners will thank you for it (one of the most beautiful cats I ever knew was eaten by a fox). Word will quickly spread among the local fox community not to go to the 'Garden of Death', and you will have achieved two things: legendary, almost godlike status among the wider fox community, and a fox-free lawn, which is nice.

It's just a thought, and no I'm not psychotic.

Billy the Bull

Hurray for pulverising our friend M le Renard. And you are so well informed. Just one question: what to do with the cadavers? Fox a l'orange?

Karaoke Girl

Nice suggestion, Billy, but I've been told that a fox's skull is extremely thick and that it requires a high-calibre rifle to kill a fox by that means. A shot to any other part of its body by an air rifle or pistol is unlikely to be truly effective most of the time. I have no axe to grind with regard to foxes vs. kittens or whatever, but I would rather that nothing dies in agony, wherever possible. We get foxes and cats in our garden and they seem to survive without conflict quite happily. So perhaps there could be another solution.

But if anybody knows how to get rid of fucking herons...

Potty Time

Herons won't go near your pond if they think that there is already another heron there. You can buy plastic herons from garden shops which do the trick, but I also heard that if you just put a football by your pond with heron markings painted on, it also deters them. Apparently they are not an intelligent bunch. Failing that, shoot the fuckers.

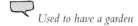

Used to have a garden

Thanks Billy, I will apply your suggestions wholeheartedly. I think you're right. Too long have I been labouring under this misapprehension that the cute little foxes have just been 'doing their own thing'. They must *die*. It's us or them. It's a man eat fox world. Where do you get small-bore weaponry in this fine city of ours?

Ad

Ad, I'm pleased you liked the idea, and in answer to your question, worryingly enough, 'Cash Converters' is a good place to look – that is, I see them for sale there lots. Also, gun shops are not as rare as you might think in this great city. However, I fear that there may be some truth in foxes' heads being more or less bullet-proof, but you can try (and you will certainly have fun). As for disposing of the bodies, the options are bounded only by your imagination: make 'lucky' key rings from their

paws – four for the price of one including bonus Davy
Crockett hat dressing (what's that all about?!) or have
them stuffed and sell them at vast profit to Islingtonites
and Hoxton dwellers, or bury them in the dead of night
in makeshift graves in St John's Wood near the clearing
where that bloke decapitated himself years ago... oh,
there I go again. Stop it stop it the voices. Seriously
though, bin 'em.

Billy the Bull

You can't shoot foxes without a licence as they aren't
classed as vermin so I wouldn't advise this course of
action unless you want to risk the boys in blue turning
up (and they carry proper guns!). I would wait until the
vixen chases the young out of the territory (you will
know when this is because suddenly the young foxes will
magically disappear and end up as roadkill). Stuff rags
dipped in Renardine down the holes which is an
effective repellent or I'm sure the Fox Project will come
round if you are too infirm or lazy or tight to sort it out
yourself. Contact them via www.foxproject.org.uk

appydaze

MICE

I recently moved out of the best bedsit in London. My best friend moved in in my place. A couple of weeks ago she met the house mouse (who used to like to drop in from time to time for a cup of tea). Best friend couldn't deal with the idea of sharing the bedsit with the mouse so she went out and bought a 'humane' mouse trap.

Best friend just sent me this email: 'Subject: the mouse is trapped – HELP!!! The mouse is in the trap and still alive – fuck! what am i gonna do now? can you come over with Kubanek? i cannot kill it while it's alive but to wait until it dies is even worse...' Kubanek, by the way, is my kitten. Obviously best friend and I will find a solution to this problem before next week's posting, but for the future, does anyone have ideas of how to dispose of mice humanely once they are trapped in those humane mouse traps? Said mousetraps contain no such instructions. They just leave the poor mouse glued to the bottom of the trap. Which is really dreadful. Thank you for your help.

mousegirl

You take aforementioned 'humane' trap containing the mouse (who I agree is probably pretty cute – until his larger less cute relations move in) up to the local park and release the mouse and then watch it overtake you on the walk home and arrive home in time to see it popping on the kettle. Believe me it takes several efforts to get rid of them – the best thing to do is really make sure that there is no food anywhere that they can get to – have stuff sealed in tins and jars and so on, and rubbish in bins with lids rather than loose in carrier bags and then they tend to move on of their own accord.

Best thing not to do is leave a huge bag of bird seed under the sink and not check it for a week only to find that the entire mouse population of south London has eaten most of the bird seed, distributed the rest all around the cupboard, has clearly thought this is the best food source since sliced bread and has called most of its friends and relations from the rest of London to share the feast. A lot of humane traps required this summer methinks! Good luck.

Katey K

I think you're supposed to release the mice on the tube or something. You could try a park but I think it would prefer the tube because the tourists feed them crisps.

Anon

My dad used to use those *humane* traps, and when he
caught a mouse, he would take it into the garden and
drown it in a bucket of water. He'd then hang it on a
tree as a warning to other mice. Not very humane, I'm
sure you'll agree, but it was quite funny (but probably
not for people who care lots about mice).

Princess Bride

Erm – next time, peanut butter might be better bait than
superglue. I'm not convinced you can call it 'humane'
otherwise. Then release the mouse far away. Preferably
someone else's garden, under cover of darkness.

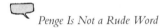
Penge Is Not a Rude Word

Mousegirl, here are my patented instructions for mouse
disposal:

1. grab mouse
2. grab hammer
3. hit mouse with hammer

I promise, he won't feel a thing!

Phesarnion

Did she seriously say 'I cannot kill it while it is alive but
cannot wait until it is dead'???! Those are indeed the
words of a hysterical girl with a mouse on her hands.
That aside, I think you need to reconsider your whole

mouse philosophy. Getting a kitten in to torment it to
death isn't really very humane, is it? But then neither is
calling your kitten Kubanek. Hmm. Anyway – why not:

1. drown it
2. stamp on it really hard (instant death)
3. set it freeeeeeee as the wind in a park somewhere (to
   go off and terrorise another bedsitter, probably)
4. get an air gun

I think mice are quite cute – I think you should go for
option 3 and give Mr Mouse a new lease of life and
possibly give somebody else the jolly good fun of
catching him in their flat. But this is a week later, so I
guess he is dead by now. May he/she rest in peace.

Braveheart

COMMON BIRDS

**I was wondering if anyone can help shed some light
on why it's been such a long time (two years at
least?) since I last saw a pair of sparrows in London.
There used to be millions of them! Now they are all
gone. There are no house martins or swallows either
for that matter, or if there are they are hiding from
me. My dad agrees (not that I consult him about
everything) and he further reckons that the seagulls
are also vanishing. So what is going on with these**

birds? Is something poisoning them or driving them away? If so, what? Why haven't all the pigeons been killed? London needs a variety of birds, not just the grimy flea-bitten pigeon monotony. Answers please if you have them.

 Billy the Bull

I consult my dad on bird matters too, and he blames domestic cats.

 *Pauline Brown*

Unfortunately urban sparrows have been declining in numbers for years (although I thought I'd seen more this year) and no one, not even Odd Billy knows why. The only excuses swallows and house martins have is that they migrate from Africa and global warming means they are crossing larger areas of desert, so more die. Adding pollution and Mediterranean 'hunters' shooting them as they pass also results in a decrease. Feral pigeons are not real birds, which is why they proliferate amongst the rubbish of the city. I bet even David Attenborough hates them. As for the gulls, really? I thought they were going strong... at least they are in Deptford.

 Big T

The reason is that the house sparrow used to live in the eaves of roofs and in hedgerow in gardens and feed from weedy areas. Since there has been an increase in house repairs and modern houses do not have accessible eaves and an increase in changing garden styles away from hedges etc., there is nowhere for them to nest. Also a decrease in the insect population in inner cities (not that you'd know it from the ant infestation I have) means less food... and this is the reason why there are fewer in the country as well. With farming methods being more efficient and the storage of grain more clinical and hygienic there is just simply not enough food. Defra produce an excellent document – have a look: www. defra.gov.uk/wildlife-countryside/ewd/sparrows.pdf.

adam

Billy the Bull – you are so right, the sparrows have emigrated because they prefer conditions in southern Europe (not sure of push factors – probably fed up with the biblical weird weather patterns and crowds and fumes). Lucky me was in Portugal in early June and there were literally THAAAASANDS of 'em tweeting and winking away like Cristiano Ronaldo himself. As for swallows and swifts, you will be pleased to hear that they do still seem to frequent the quieter pools and streams and even the A232 Sutton–Croydon stretch of our native land. For less suspect bird knowledge, log onto the RSPB's website and check out 'BirdWeb', which tracks and surveys sparrows among other feathered friends. www.rspb.org.uk/science/birdweb.

Snickers

Apparently this is simply due to the death of the Horse and Cart. The little fellow used to feed on the horse feed, which contained a high amount of various seeds. So obviously when the Horse and Cart method of transport declined, so did their food source and the poor little blighters probably died in their thousands due to mass competition. I also think that people generally don't put out as much food as they used to.

James Evans

People have lost sight of the important role magpies play in attacking the nests of other British birdlife. I don't know if they are protected species or not but someone needs to reduce their numbers in and around the Barbican. Oh, and skateboarders are a nuisance too.

Keyworker

I live right near London Bridge and I have loads in my garden, though to my shock a kestrel picked a couple off

while they were having their lunch. Amazing. I also
have green finch, jay, blue tits and more.

twitcher

Billy mate. Where do you live? In a cellar? I have found
that, when seeking our feathered pals, it is handy to look
in the sky. I'll put you in touch with a mate of mine who
has been driving me nuts for the last few weeks by
constantly pointing out swallows, house martins and
swifts just so he can show how feckin clever he is at
telling the difference. Of course this doesn't really work
when his audience (a) don't give a shit and (b) wouldn't
know the difference if he bullshitted his way through
it... which I wouldn't put past him. Anyway, loads in
West London. Come have a look.

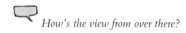

How's the view from over there?

The drastic drop in sparrow numbers has been in the
news for around ten years now. The *Independent* offered
a cash prize for anyone who could work out why they
have practically disappeared from London, after numbers
fell by 50% in cities between 1970 and 2000. When they
started this, some cities in Europe still had lots but the
bad news is that there has now been a similar fall in Paris,
Rome and other cities in Europe. Don't be fooled
because you see some around this time of year. It seems
that there are more around at the start of summer. By the

end of summer, you'll see hardly any at all in London. Personally, I'm really sad about this. I've always been fond of sparrows but I did kind of take them for granted, thinking they'd always be around wherever you went. I've started to appreciate starlings and swifts and swallows much more now – maybe they'll be next?

billy

EXOTIC BIRDS

I have just rescued a parakeet from Kensington Gardens... Big up for the Parakeets!

Yes Way

Were those parakeets bright green with red beaks? If so, they're part of the burgeoning (7000-strong and climbing) south west London wild parakeet population that reputedly can trace their lineage back to a breeding pair released into the wild by Jimi Hendrix in the hope they would make Swinging London more colourful. Now, while I don't believe the Hendrix connection, I can vouch for the existence of the wild parakeets, three or four of which regularly appear at the bird feeder in my garden in Tooting. They are also feisty little beggars, capable of putting up quite a fight against the pesky squirrels who think the feeder is actually theirs. For more information on London's wild parakeet colonies look here: www.vino.demon.co.uk/fong/parak.html.

auawsha

Just as an aside – a friend told me she'd seen the parrots in Brockwell Park, so they are spreading east!

Ginja Ninja

A whole troop of the little sods roost in a graveyard near Kilburn and then en masse swoop over Kilburn and West Hampstead squawking their inane little heads off. Can everyone buy a cat? Ooooh... and miniature helicopters (for the cats obviously).

how's the view from over there?

No sooner had I read this than I looked out of my bathroom window and there are parakeets flying over and landing in and around the gardens of Abbey Wood.

Jonesy

The parakeets were seen in Crayford and Sidcup (Bexley London Borough) years ago and were featured on *Newsroom South East* as a novelty news article. Now they are everywhere...

Bobbers

In spite of their loudness and shitability, I think that
these troops of green parakeets make our daily, normal,
routine and slightly boring London a little bit more
exotic. Do you get gangs of wild parakeets flying around
any other English, Scottish or Welsh city? So you've got
fewer sparrows, but maybe a few more green parakeets –
it balances out...

Me 2

ROOS AND WALLABIES

**A couple of months ago my girlfriend was driving
me back to the airport at 4 a.m. All of a sudden I saw
from the corner of my eye a kangaroo. My girlfriend
insists that I probably saw a fox. (Are foxes grey?)
Please can anyone confirm my story? Has anyone
seen a kangaroo in London (outside of a zoo)?**

dutch boyfriend

You'd think this fella was on drugs wouldn't you, but
amazingly there have been reported sightings of 'roos in
the UK (mostly, by worse for wear Aussies, to be fair).
Still, a number of wallabies are soon to be resident in
Kew Gardens so maybe you had a vision...

Juvey

You might not be crazy – a dead marsupial was found on the M40 in Buckinghamshire a few years ago.

bushmonkey

Wallabies. There are loads of them living semi-wild in the Home Counties regions. I know that one lot escaped from captivity near Henley about 25 years ago, and they've now spread along the M40 corridor. There is also an established bunch of wallabies in Horsham. So with luck and no small determination on their part, within a few years, the streets of London could be at the mercy of communities of hardened, cynical urban wallabies, eating flowerbeds, scrumping apples and making 'street drinkers' do that hilarious double-take-throw-the-bottle-away thing they do in movies.

Portland Place Bill

HORSES

My mate used to live in Chalk Farm and I woke up there to the sound of horses hooves at about 6 in the morning. I looked out the window to see hundreds of horses just strolling up the street on their own. Where do they come from? The zoo doesn't have that many horses so the only other explanation we could come up with is police or army but surely

you'd notice anywhere that could keep that many horses in central London?

Splat

The horses come from the Regent's Park/St John's Wood Barracks. Although it may seem as if they were out and about by themselves, there are riders with them. A couple in front, some dotted through the middle and some bringing up the rear. I used to watch them from my bedroom window as a young 'un, and now I watch them with my grandson. Ah, the good ol' days...

thats me in the corner

COWS

After the Great Fire in 1666 it was made illegal to have thatched roofs in London, so how come the _Globe_ on the South Bank has got a thatched roof? Also, can I still graze cows on common land like Wandsworth Common? If so, where can I buy a cow from? How much are they and how pissed off will people be with me grazing it on various sites across London?

Roger Persang

You should be able to get most of a cow from Smithfield's, but I doubt it would do much grazing.

Mooo

Alas Wandsworth Common is not common land but is owned by the council. I've heard tell that cows can be bought in a strange muddy place called 'The Country' or swapped for a bag of magic beans.

auawsha

The *Globe's* thatched roof is the first to be built in central London since the Great Fire, and had to have special permission from the authorities. If you have a look at the top of the thatch it's got special Tudor sprinkler systems set up as well.

Abi

If you are anywhere near Epping Forest there are cows that enjoy ancient grazing rights and stray all over the fucking road, so why not just purloin one? You will need (a) a large shot of cow tranquilliser, (b) a steady nerve and (c) a large vehicle to convey said animal, but it deserves a thought.

pussinboots

Is there any common land left in London??

sweet fa

I hear that South London is quite common.

Kensington Chappie

PLACES

L ONDON IS... PLACES TO SIT QUIET AND watch the world go by; places half-hidden or scarily high; London is places to walk, woo and wee; London is burlesque and Battersea; London is places to celebrate every key moment of your life, every weekend and every spare hour; London is places you'll never, ever forget...

What's the most invigorating thing about London?
'I like the fact you can find shops that sell nothing but cheese, green biros and strange Japanese omelette pans. *The Tate.* I like the parks being so close to the busy bits, but what's really exciting is the constant bubbling of the underworld – I like the feeling that there's naughty stuff going on, that you could turn a corner and come across a bar for flesh-eating zombies or something, and I love it right now, in summer, when everyone seems happier and everything looks lovely, and it's the best place to be in the world... oh dammit, but I'm leaving on Saturday...'

 *Will Rankin*, adventurer

PLACES TO PONDER

PEACEFUL PLACES

Does anyone here have somewhere in the city they like to go to sit alone with their thoughts or perhaps read a book? I've become very fond of the courtyards at Broadgate, particularly the one behind Liverpool Street station. There's nothing like strolling through the city at 5 a.m. on a weekend (or a weekday if you're feeling adventurous), getting a takeaway breakfast from *Ponti's* cafe and heading for Broadgate to sit with your thoughts by the fountain. The best bit is you can see into Liverpool Street station and watch as the trains are silently organised for the next day of operation. Blissful.

Enfant

I find that a bench on the South Bank facing St Paul's is an excellent zone-out area, especially early in the day before it gets too mental. Also, on nice days I like to sit at Finsbury Circus with a potboiler...

Mamfer

I don't know where you are based, but *Marylebone Parish Church* (on Marylebone Road) has a nice garden just behind the church, as does *St Johns* at Hampstead and *St Giles in the Fields* just off Charing Cross Road. The City of London has a dozen or more pretty planted spaces, often where churches used to be, pre-WW2, where flowers and sandwiches can be enjoyed without much interruption from traffic. Then there's Lincoln Inn Fields, Gray's Inn Gardens, and the Middle Temple, with its lovely fountain.

grave lounger

There is a church in Knightsbridge called *Holy Trinity Brompton*. It has a large grounds open to the public, with trees and birds and squirrels. It is beautiful and very, very peaceful. Here for addresses and whatnot: www.htb.org.uk/

Bo Jaxx

Whilst Bo Jaxx's suggestion of *Holy Trinity* is indeed a good one, I assume that you mean The City. Possibly the nicest place in or around the square mile is Postman's Park near St Bart's hospital. Back in the days when I could leave the office for a lunch break it was a popular place to go on sunny days. Info can be found here: www.thejoyofshards.co.uk/london/tiles/ppark/index.shtml

Enjoy it and think of me stuck at my desk.

Custard

HIDDEN PLACES

I'm after a challenge to visit some of the hidden London landmarks that normally get overlooked. Things like Karl Marx's grave. Any ideas?

Garkbit

One of London's hidden gems is the *Bank of England Museum*. It's small, you can go around it in an hour easily. It's free – kinda odd for a bank. The only drawback is that it's open only during the day on Monday to Friday – no evenings and no weekends. But if any readers are in the area and have a bit of time to kill, I recommend it.

Evil Dave

You could try looking for the bank that installed the world's first ATM machine. Apparently it's the Barclays in Enfield.

craven maven

In Stratford, where I live, is a Cleopatra's Needle-shaped monument to one Samuel Gurney. Who he? He's a long-dead prison reformer, who was married to the more famous Elizabeth Fry.

Zabadak

I have just finished reading *Underground London* by Stephen Smith, and he visits a multitude of really interesting historic sites in London that are overlooked quite often I would imagine, as most can be found underground.

cybermunkee

I don't know if this is really what you're after, Garkbit, but others might find it interesting anyway. I remember reading about Parkland Walk, possibly on some blog; there were photos and it looked really interesting and I thought to myself I really must go and investigate. Have I? Have I f★ck! That was probably about three or four years ago. Anyway, if you're less lazy than me, and it sounds like you are, Parkland Walk is basically an old disused railway line that runs across North London. You can apparently walk from Highgate station (Marx's grave nearby of course, which is what reminded me of it) to Finsbury Park, and barely see a road! From what I remember, there's lots of interesting things along the way too. Find it on Google Maps, put it on Hybrid mode and you can see what I mean from satellite, which will probably be the closest I ever get to it now I'm a Balhambrian and almost as lazy as when I lived in Camden.

uberrich

This isn't really 'hidden' I suppose but I think *St Giles Church* in Cripplegate is really interesting. It's at the Barbican and amidst all the modern buildings there is this old church (where Oliver Cromwell was married) and part of the Roman Wall still exists.

Enfieldian chick

I've spent quite a lot of time looking for hidden London for my job, but the only 'oh my God I just don't believe it' moment so far was finding the *Buddhapadipa Thai* temple amongst the mediumly posh houses around Wimbledon Common.

But if it's Communist leaders you want, you could also try the *Marx Memorial Library*, see the room where Lenin designed Communism and behold a mural of a giant oppressed worker casting off his Stanley Spencer-esque chains. It's open to the public between 1 and 2, I think (and it's in a very attractive square in Clerkenwell with a nice pub and teashops): www.marxlibrary.net.

museumkate

museumkate is right, the Buddhist temple in
Wimbledon is indeed impressive. In a similar vein, but
from a different part of the world, regular drivers on the
London-inbound section of the M4 will know the
Russian Orthodox Church, a stone's throw from
Gunners-bury tube. It's in Harvard Road, W4. It's like
being in St Petersburg or Moscow!

robram

Not quite hidden London owing to its size but around
the corner from the North Circular between Neasden
and *Ikea*, and in the middle of a residential estate you will
find a colossal Hindu temple.

Shelley

Well this is slightly hidden... *Merton Abbey Mills*, which
used to be the *William Morris Print Works*. There is a very
nice market there at weekends, plus a nice pub which is
great in summer to just sit and watch the river over a
cold pint. It also used to be the site of an old abbey
(strangely enough); you can still see some of the ruins of
the priory under the bridge between the market and
Sainsbury's. Typically they've built on the rest of the
ruins. If you fancy a walk you can follow the river
upstream, which will take you past a city farm and
quite a few National Trust parks and eventually
Croydon. Or downstream, where you'll end up at the

soon-to-be-closed *Young's Brewery* in Wandsworth. See
www.mertonabbeymills.com.

Stiltskin

One of the delightful little surprises in the City of
London is Postman's Park on Aldersgate Street, just
before the *Museum of London*. It's almost quiet in there.
Also while you're there, wander down to the NCP car
park in London Wall, and marvel at the fact that they
built over and around a 2000-year-old relic. Jeez, I'm on
a roll now. If you're enjoying your Saturday stroll
around the City, then wander up to Moorgate and head
north for a visit to Bunhill Fields where you'll find the
Dissenter's Graveyard where various luminaries are
entombed. Once fully rested head west once more and
have a spot of lunch/dinner at the *Café Du Marche*. Fair
enough, not a typical British restaurant, but the location
always makes me feel like I've stumbled on one of
London's secrets. Oh, have the cheese too. Magic!

Juvey

PHOTOGENIC PLACES

**As a keen photographer, I've just upgraded to a
rather spiffing DSLR camera, and now I'm looking
for Londony inspiration for weekend photographic
jaunts. I would be really chuffed if anyone could
recommend places, areas or things that might be**

interesting to shoot – I'm especially interested in fading or decaying things (old stations, adverts, closed shops...) and industrial architecture – station roofs etc. Bonus points for anyone who recommends somewhere where I won't get mugged the minute I whip my camera out.

Ker-chick

Dunno if anyone has sent this before but this site has lots of photos and stories about derelict buildings around London. See how many pubs you know! www.derelictlondon.com.

Dicko

There's a very colourful, interesting building on the corner of Eastcheap and Philpot Lane in the city. Unfortunately the bottom floor is a Coffee Nerds shop, but if you look up it really is lovely. I often see walking tour groups being told all about it, but I've never had enough time to linger and listen.

CityBoy

On the corner of Cato Road and Clapham High Street there's an architect's office that looks like a cross between a swimming pool and the inside of an underground station. I asked one of the architects who works there what the building used to be and apparently it was one of around five 'dry' pool halls built around London years ago in an attempt to give men something to do other than drink ale at night. He also thought that the rest of them had been demolished and that this was the last one standing. It's not grand or shiny or pretty, but I think it's lovely.

GA

Conkers
Autumn's nearly here, where's the best place to get conkers in London then?

spaniel

Trees are a good place to look. Or the ground underneath trees. Although I prefer hanging around outside school gates and making small children turn out their pockets. Sometimes I just turn them upside down and shake them a bit till the conkers fall out. You have to be careful though. I ended up covered in sherbet yesterday.

Curry Mile

HIGH PLACES

I've got a bit of thing about standing on top of really high places and looking at the view. Paris has the *Eiffel Tower*, New York has got the *Empire State Building* but where do I go in London? I've been to the champagne bar at the top of *Tower 42* but it's hilariously expensive to buy a drink, and they won't let you just sit and gorm out of the window. Similar thing with the *Eye*, you only get half an hour... any ideas?

spaniel

Let's sort this into three categories:

Buildings open to the public...

1. *Peckham Library* is an amazing building in itself but if you go to the top floors you get an absolutely fantastic view of London. I'm sure the windows must be polarised or something, because the views are so clear. And there's also an eel, pie and mash shop very nearby.
2. The *Mayor's Office/City Hall.* About one weekend every month the building is open to the public – there's no need to book, just walk in and go to the top floor where there is a fantastic view of the city. Afterwards, make sure you go to the basement where there is a huge floor map of Greater London.

It's quite fun to find your own home and stand on it (or someone else's).

3. The viewing gallery at *Tate Modern*, but it's only on the fourth floor which is a little low for you.

4. The *OXO Building* on the South Bank. There's a viewing gallery on the very top floor which has great views of the City.

5. *Westminster Cathedral* (the Roman Catholic one) in Victoria. It's much easier and cheaper to go to the top of this cathedral than it is at St Paul's. Just go through the front door and take the lift to the top (I think it costs about 50p).

6. The *Monument* costs £2 and everyone should go to the top at least once, but it's one of those things that Londoners never do. You'd expect it to be blocked in by all the big buildings in the City but the view is good.

7. *Marble Arch* is run by English Heritage, and you can go to the rooftop. The unique selling point here is that you can see directly into *Buckingham Palace*'s back garden, including their tennis court which I never knew was there.

Bars...

1. Just off Langham Place is *St George's Hotel*, and when you go into the foyer go to the lifts and go directly to the *Heights Bar*. The drinks are reasonably priced and the view is good on both sides of the room; the

windows are very large and run right around the bar. The staff are friendly, and since it's used a lot by the BBC then whatever you wear you'll fit right in with management, creatives or actors.

2. I've heard the *Hilton Hotel* in Kensington is relaxed and has a great view, but I've never been there myself.

Outside spaces...

1. *Parliament Hill*, naturally.
2. *Greenwich Hill* as well. This may be the best view in London. Someone once told me that views looking north are better than views looking south because the sun is behind you and the shadows and contrast are better. Why don't you go and see if he was right?

Hope this helps.

Eclectic Angel

The *Royal Observatory* in Greenwich has *amazing* views of London, my favourite view in fact. You could also try sneaking in to high-rise council blocks. They usually have 'tradesman' buttons that are switched on between 8 a.m. and 11 a.m. You obviously want one that has windows in the communal parts of the building.

Babb

All you need to do is find a nice high block and go to the top! A lot of them have entry systems so wait for someone to go in or alternatively, buzz a random number telling them you're the police, or a plumber or postman and are trying to get to the house next door. You are then free to travel all the way up to the top floor and stare out the window for as long as takes your fancy!

Feetfirmlyonthefloor

For London views from up high, I've always enjoyed going up to the *Kensington Roof Gardens* (www.roofgardens.com) – pretty fine views of London a mere stone's throw from High Street Ken. Not many people know about them (well a few more people do now, I guess) and you get the joy of seeing panoramic London in the company of the resident flamingos (yep, real ones). Once you're done, you can go into Kensington, find a café and stuff your face whilst observing the area's other wildlife – Sloaney ponies.

BC – The 'getting high' geek

It is almost like the *Monument* is invisible to Londoners. I worked near there for two months and never saw anyone go up there without the rucksack and anorak combo, which is the exact opposite of what you want to be wearing when everyone has to squeeze past everyone on the narrow stairs. Buck the trend, go up the tower in your work togs, pay the price of a sandwich, get an amazing view of the city from its centre, and a certificate when you come down (yes, really). I keep mine with my degree.

justbackfromturkey

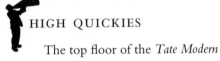

HIGH QUICKIES

The top floor of the *Tate Modern*

Wooden(high)Horse

The eighteenth floor of *New Zealand House*

Haymarket – Flo

The top of *Centrepoint*, Oxford Street

Zabadak

The *Tavistock Clinic*, junction of Belsize Lane and Fitzjohn's Avenue

wicked witch of the west end

The very top of *St Paul's Cathedral*

Bo Tocks

OPEN PLACES

Every year I read about the wonderful *Open House Weekend* where we can peek behind the scenes at some of the wondrous closed buildings of London. This year I'm determined to have a shufti. I want to know if any fellow LbLers have ever gone through the keyhole, so to speak, and have any recommendations. I live south east, although am happy to go central.

robram

My best bit of advice to you is not to overstretch yourself. A lot of the places have limited opening hours during the weekend and rushing across the city to a timetable is an extra stress you probably don't want or need. Some of the best places I've visited on *Open House Weekend* have been ones where I've just walked past and noticed the green *Open House* poster outside. A prime example of this is *St Ann's Church* in Soho where you can go up the narrowest of narrow staircases to the clock tower. Other cracking places include *St Pancras Chambers*, *Freemasons' Hall*, the top of *Ken's Testicle*, *The Old Operating Theatre*, 19 Princelet Street and some of the gentlemen's clubs on Pall Mall. My dad has rudely arranged his sixtieth birthday for this weekend so enjoy London and think of me while I'm being asked by elderly aunts why I'm not married yet.

Joe Moon

To get the best from *Open House Weekend*, get yourself a copy of the *Open House* guide (from your local library or bigger bookshops). What's worth seeing depends on what type of buildings or period in history interests you. To my mind, the stars are the modern private homes, and some of the government buildings. A very short list of suggestions:

City of London – *The Guildhall*; *Lloyds of London*; *Great Eastern Hotel*; *Liverpool Street station*

Camden – the *Chapel* and new *Orangery* at Great Ormond Street Hospital; *The Art Workers Guild*, Queen Square; *Freemasons' Hall*, Covent Garden

Westminster – *Foreign Office and HM Treasury*, 44 Berkeley Square; *The Lansdowne Club*; *Channel 4 TV*; *RSA*, off the Strand; *The Royal Courts of Justice*, the Strand

You didn't say where in the SE you live, so:

Greenwich – *Charlton House*, 89 Genesta Road, SE18

Lambeth – *Ritzy Cinema*, Brixton

Lewisham – *Ecological House*, SE23

Southwark – *Peckham Library*; *William Booth College*; Denmark Hill for the climb up the tower

Putney regular Open House go-er and volunteer guide

Yes, I'm one of those alien life forms who visit this website but don't actually live in London (not to mention the fact that I'm also probably 20+ years older than the average LbLer). Anyway, read about the *Open House Weekend* in a previous post and happened to be down in London on the Saturday, so gave it a go.

Had a brilliant day – *Almeida Theatre*, *Great Eastern Hotel*, *Lloyd's*, *St Ethelburga*'s (particularly poignant in view of recent events). Everyone I met either queuing or shepherding was without exception polite, helpful and knowledgeable. So thanks very much for the recommendation.

yorkshirelass

Places to party

QUIRKY PLACES

A mate of mine took me to the *Ice Bar* this week which was a really cool night out. Anyway I said I would take him somewhere equally as weird and quirky but I'm struggling to think of anywhere. Any suggestions?

law

Hey law, nice pun. Not sure that anywhere's going to match the quirkiness of the *Ice Bar*, but I might be able to do slightly eccentric, if not outright quirky. It means coming out east to Hoxton/Shoreditch (are these place names completely interchangeable or is there a distinction?), but it's better than the West End anyway. I digress. To the point: try out *LoungeLover* – www.loungelover.co.uk – just off Bethnal Green Road. It's very opulent and pretty poncy (but then I like that). So poncy in fact, that you can't order drinks from the bar, even if you're leant against it all night (which is quite likely as getting a table is, or used to be, nigh on impossible unless you book). You have to order from waiting staff that float around. Anyway, it's definitely an experience. Suggest going there towards the beginning of the evening for two or three sharpeners, before repairing to some other Shoreditch hostelry. The reason being that (a) you'll appreciate the excellent cocktails if you're (more or less) sober and (b) it's a tad pricey (circa ten quid a pop).

uberrich

The *Ice Bar* is not 'cool', not in any but the most literal sense. It is more like a distinctly undelicious melange of a battery farm and Hitler's Bunker. Worse still, you can only stay in there for about half an hour before you start losing your toes.

Bo Jaxx

Quirky? I'll give you quirky: *Dream Bags Jaguar Shoes*. Search it.

I can add no more.

Stevedore from Tyneside

I have just come across eating in the pitch black at *Dans Le Noir*: www.danslenoir.com

The following description is from *Daily Candy*: 'You order food on arrival before being led to your table by a partially sighted or blind member of staff. Sample unseen delights like Three Tastes of Salmon or tournedos with shallot mousseline and horseradish crisps. When you've come to your senses at the end of the meal, you can discuss the experience with fellow eaters-in-the-dark in a well-lit lounge. You'll be surprised by all the new sensations that have been stirred up'.

milkandtwo

Quirky, hmmmmmmm. I'm not sure if this is what you're after but there is a place called *Bar Vinyl* in Camden Town. It seems really great for people who like music, with an amazing record shop where you can take your pint and have a gander. DJs start from 2 and are usually vvv good. Enjoy.

knowledge(less)

Nice of knowledge(less) to recommend *Bar Vinyl*, but if you do go there, don't sit near the door, or the little gang of scum who hang around by the market outside will steal your bag, like they did my girlfriend's as we sat there enjoying a nice drink and a tasty snack...

Horns

Try *Coffee Cake and Kink*, Endell Street, Covent Garden. It's a coffee bar, shop, downstairs lounge and gallery serving coffee (obviously!) and erotica. Upstairs, books are laid on tables for you to browse through while the downstairs lounge is more interesting, with alcoves, display cabinets and photographic exhibits. It's a good mixed crowd but probably a little more Kinky than Quirky!

Miss Rah

**Party destination for
25 good-time gals**
*The second Saturday in February, 25
good-time gals need suggestions for a
party destination in east/central
London. We'll be dressed as hip-hop ladies from the
1980s, à la Salt n Pepa, in rolled-up dungarees and
baggy Ts. Somewhere large enough to allow us to
blend in would be ideal. And with music similar to the
playlist at* Guilty Pleasures.

Karaoke Girl

*Just make it anywhere other than where I intend to be,
which is the excellent-looking 'Down with Valentines'*
Feeling Gloomy *night at the* Islington Bar Academy:
www.feelinggloomy.com. *I will be in the bar, with my
head on the bar, if any LbLers would care to join me.
Past FGs have been wonderful. If there's one thing
I can't stand it's big groups of drunken people in
uniform fancy dress. Still, kudos for originality and not*

going for angel wings and devil horns. Have a great evening!

Drumbo

BURLESQUE PLACES

I've read with interest that burlesque nights are making a comeback; a friend of mine went to the 'Whoopie Club' at the *Hackney Empire*. It sounds like just the ticket for a fun night out, but I can't find details of any upcoming events in London. Does anyone have any suggestions of websites or venues to try?

babybat

Don't know of any comprehensive listings for burlesque but if babybat wants to learn the basics of burlesque, or how to remove a glove or twirl a nipple tassle then the International Workshop Festival opens very soon with short courses. There is also a evening of burlesque films with live performances: www.workshopfestival.co.uk.

Tikki

A number of clubs in London should satisfy the needs of a prospective burlesque fan. Some are about dressing up and having a good dance; some are about unusual cabaret performances; and others provide a good meal as well as a show. Eras from the 1920s to the 1950s are evoked across the various organisations represented in this list:

www.themoderntimesclub.co.uk

www.ladyluckclub.co.uk

www.thewhoopeeclub.com

www.theflashmonkey.biz

www.theredrat.com

www.lostvagueness.com

www.clubmontepulciano.com

www.a1people.com/cathouse.html

www.virginiacreepersclub.co.uk

www.mediumrare.tv

www.duckie.co.uk

www.shunt.co.uk.

Edwardian

PLACES TO GET 'MESSY'

Just wondering if anybody knows anywhere in London where people can get deep down and messy, i.e. a pie fight and other messy activities?

Miles

Miles, there is a group of people that organise pillow fights – the last one was outside *St Paul's*. Perhaps we could get them to organise another, have Round One with pillows and then Round Two with pies, mushy peas and even gravy. Then, to rinse, have a third round with water balloons.

Need a good old punch up

How about the food hall in *Harrods*? They have their own pies you know.

spaniel

I saw an article in a magazine recently about a pub that has frequent nights involving piss-play, where everyone wees over one another and gets very messy. It's near either the Elephant or Vauxhall. I'll find out for you. It's definitely in south London, and I think it's a fiver to get in.

Tris2000

Central Station in King's Cross has a night called 'Streams of Pleasure' or 'SOP' on Thursdays if you really wanna get wee'd on. Never go on a Friday though 'cause it smells like – well, like a toilet!

Oh, this is all of course 'so I've heard'.

dryasabone

WTF?! Miles, explain, is that what you were alluding to in your original post? Being wee'd on? God, I feel so innocent and naïve at times...

(wanders off to look at some bloke's puppies)

spaniel

No, I don't mean 'Streams of Pleasure' or any of that stuff (ugh!). I mean getting messy with custard pies and other sweet foodstuffs in a group type situation – you know, like 'Bugsy Malone'.

Miles

Check out *Splosh* magazine. Specialist fetish mag for messy stuff with custard, chocolate sauce, beans etc... They may have some events planned (I'm not subscriber, so haven't a clue).

notacreampieinsight

Quotidian Places

PLACES TO WALK

I've decided to get to know the great Londres better by going one of these walking tour things. But, there are *hundreds*! So can anyone recommend one or two? Always seems that the guide themselves is the most important part, so do name names. I'm quite taken with idea of a ghost walk or Jack the Ripper type thing... but then I might get scared!

FabSal

As a non-Londoner and thus entitled to behave like a tourist and admit my lack of knowledge about London, I have been on lots of London guided walks and have never suffered a boring one. I've done quite a few with the *Original London Walks* (they have the black and white pamphlet you can appropriate from any hotel foyer).

yorkshirelass

I've enjoyed the walks by London Walks (www.walks. com). I went on the 'Spies and Spycatchers' London' last Saturday and had a blast. We went through St James's and Mayfair – two areas I've walked past, but never really explored fully. The guide was Alan. I think he does a number of walks for the company. Pick a walk that goes through a part of London you've never seen and have fun!

Veronica

While the evenings are still dark, you should definitely go on a Jack the Ripper walk – we went on the one run by www.walks.com with the author Donald Rumbelow doing the talking – it's a busy patch and we bumped into two or three other Ripper tours, but found people migrating to ours as this guy really knows what he's talking about (he's consulted on a number of films including *From Hell* – 'interesting theory but actually rubbish, I told them, but...', he said). Walks are about two hours and do check the note on the site about getting the right one – Donald wore a sinister-looking fedora hat which rather added to the mystery and ambiance of the evening! No need to book, just turn up at Tower Hill tube at the appointed hour – the site tells you which days Donald is working. Take a tenner and he'll sign and sell you a copy of his latest book.

Mainmenu

I've done the Ripper one and found it excellent (although I think one needs to bear in mind that we are looking at a series of murder sites, lest we think of them as simple tourist attractions). Our guide was Donald

Rumbelow, who is considered a world authority on J
the R. Very good.

Declan

I'd strongly recommend both of the *Time Out London
Walks* books. A couple of years ago, when I wasn't
working, I kept myself sane and fit, and explored
London by following the walks in these books. Each
book features 25 or 30 walks, written by London
luminaries, including Arthur Smith, Graham Norton,
Sue Arnold and others, and they show you round their
favourite parts of London. I discovered so many great
museums, pubs and parks by following these walks, so
I'd recommend this DIY option to anyone!

Dan

PLACES TO WOO

**I want to take my girlfriend on a whirlwind winter
romantic tour of London in the week before
Christmas, just so we can gawp at the pretty
Christmas lights and hopefully she'll start to realise
just what I love about London. Aside from ice-skating
at *Somerset House* Ice Rink, do you have any other
great romantic suggestions that'll just melt her heart?**

almost witty

Why not try taking her to West India Quay, they've got some beautiful Christmas trees and big snowmen and there's a lovely tapas restaurant where you could take her for dinner. Alternatively try the *Gun* pub at Coldharbour. Its terrace overlooks the Thames and the water comes right up. It's beautiful at night and has roaring fires; you don't feel like you're in London at all.

Crofty

Just take a walk along the south side of the Thames, starting at Waterloo (perhaps go on the *London Eye*?) then continue eastwards, taking in *Tate Modern* (which might be open so you can pop inside), Gabriel's Wharf, the *Globe Theatre*, the no-longer wobbly bridge, which is worth walking across to get fantastic views along the Thames and a marvellous view of *St Paul's*, then back again, then into the *Anchor Bankside* for a swift one, then carry on to the replica of the *Golden Hinde* which is in dry dock. Then past *Southwark Cathedral*, past the *Glass Testicle*, under Tower Bridge, through the old spice area past *La Pont de la Tour* (lovely smells) and then have a pizza at *Ask Pizzas* (they're always good) and see if you can get a window table so that when you're not gazing lovingly at each other, you can enjoy the view. This is one of my favourite strolls. Hope that helps.

PottyTime

PLACES TO WEE

**After being caught short recently in London Bridge,
failing utterly to manage to use the two public
conveniences near platform 12 – which never *ever*
seem to be working – I got to thinking. Maybe we
should compile a list of real conveniences – places
that Londoners can pee for free. *Borders* bookshops
were always rather good, but a lot of them seem to
have now limited access to people who have actually
bought something. I think the one on Oxford Street
is still free though. Also, large branches of Marks
and Spencer are always good for a happy slash.
Anywhere else?**

Bo Jaxx

Totally agree, Bo Jaxx. I'm a bit of a Mr Weak Bladder
meself (not saying you have a weak bladder – more of a
self-admission!). Anyway, I'll add *House of Fraser* to your
starter for ten. Although considering they're meant to be
a bit upmarket, the loos are proper skanky. But yo!
where are disabled Londoners sposed to pee (*House of
Fraser* and *Marks* excluded)??

See: www.free2pee.org.uk.

Hairy Leper

Selfridges have free, clean toilets.

NikNaks

You could try the pavement, Ramillies Street (just off Oxford Street) – that's where everyone else goes. Don't worry, the Council disinfects the place about once a month.

Caught Short

Head up to Platform 5 at London Bridge where there is a public convenience for you to happy slash to your heart's content. It does stink (the gents, I can't speak for the ladies), but it beats limping along with a bursting bladder.

Forest Hill Billy

I've become rather an expert on free toilets in the capital thanks to a dicky bladder. Most large pubs are fairly easy to use without buying a drink. The massive *Wetherspoons* in Kingsway, Holborn for instance. Others include *World's End* in Camden, the *Roundhouse* in Highgate, and the *Pint Pot* in Tottenham Court Road. There's also a permanently packed pub on the corner of Oxford Street and Tottenham Court Road whose name I forget that's easy to use too. You might also want to try

Paperchase in Tottenham Court Road and *Waterstones* in Piccadilly. Don't forget all the big art galleries.

Bunky

I always use the loos in museums or galleries when I'm caught short in town. They're free and always clean and pleasant. You may even get a bit of culture while you piss. The *V&A* is a particular favourite and of course the *National Gallery* is very handy for central London.

Raffers

The ubiquitous *Starbucks*. Though I do weaken and buy a rocky road on the way out.

Heavens

Don't forget the omnipresent *McDonald's*, *KFCs* and *Burger Kings*. To be frank, the only reason I have ever been to any of these in the last couple of years was because I wanted to use their washroom facilities.

Tintin

Not of any real use, I know, but I remember reading (in *Viz?*) that nipping into *McDonald's* with the sole intention of using their toilet is known as a 'McShit'. If you are collared by a member of their staff who tells you that

the toilets are for customer use only you should placate
them by promising to buy some food afterwards. This, in
turn, is called a 'McShit with Lies'. Um, as you were...

bandrew

SPECIAL OCCASION
PLACES

BIRTHDAY PARTIES

Birthdays. More often than not, they simply involve
'drinks' and a night out. Now I'm all for a bit of
drinkage but surely there's a better way to spend a
birthday and involve everyone so that the groups of
people who have never met can actually interact
with each other? It seems if you're not almost dead
from a hangover the next day, you didn't have a
good birthday. Tish tosh tash to that, I say! So what
I was thinking of (and admittedly my birthday isn't
until early next year) was doing something fun with
a capital F. Like laser quest, quasar or paintball, or
karting, or a river trip with a twist or a giant game of
Twister etc. Well, maybe not the Twister but you
get the idea. The only restriction is that it can't be

ludicrously expensive. Suggestions welcome one and all!

Ego sum mercator

For my thirtieth, I decided to be different and hark back to my childhood by having a game of rounders in Victoria Park. Darn good fun, reminded me of times when I used to watch *Why Don't You?* (jeez that was bad) and had a crowd of late 20/30 somethings shouting 'Rounder, rounder'. Excellent fun, and the only cost was the £15 I spent on the rounders bat and ball at *John Lewis*.

Another idea was my best mate's thirtieth the previous week, where a bunch of us went wakeboarding down at Thorpe Park – £30 for the afternoon and a BBQ thrown in to boot. We still got trollied after both events, but hey, we tried! All you need to do is hope your birthday's not in the dark winter months and you're on to a winner!

BC – The Alternative Birthday Celebration Geek

I recently had a fabulous night out with a group of friends at the roller disco behind King's Cross – www.rollerdisco.info/home.htm – only £12.50 including skate hire. The drinks are a bit pricey but you can't have too many anyways, otherwise you'd be in danger of doing some serious damage!!

redhead showgirl

Have you tried *Namco Station*? Next to the *Aquarium* on the South Bank? Dodgems, ten-pin bowling, air hockey, fairground games, racing games, loads of games. And a bar. I've actually spent a couple of happy birthdays in there, mainly getting bruises on the dodgem cars.

child@heart

Craft Night – get that nasty hangover but make something fun at the same time – and it's only a fiver. There's one on the first Monday of every month at the Notting Hill Arts Club. Or, paint while you drink! It's a bit pricey at £40 per person, but for that you get an easel, paint and a canvas for you to ejaculate your creative juices over: www.fig108.com.

the figurative pineapple

I totally echo your thoughts. I've also got to the point where I need a change from just glugging away in the pub for that special occasion. So I went to see *Chinese Elvis* at the *Drunken Monkey* bar in Hoxton instead! Still involved booze and mates but also 'The King' and great music. Top stuff!

chillisaucesalad

How about hiring a Karaoke Room in *Gallery Rendezvous* on Beak Street? You and your friends get your own private room and karaoke facilities to make complete tits out of yourselves (but only in front of each other!). Call 020 7437 4446 if you're interested.

Also, *Urban Golf* on Great Pulteney Street. You can pick any course in the world and it comes up on a screen in front of you which you can whack your balls at, from green, rough. It's a great day or night out and something a bit different: www.urbangolf.co.uk.

spandandgle

If there's a big crowd and it's a big birthday you could organise a Monopoly treasure hunt around London then end up swapping stories in the pub (give each team a disposable camera and they have to have the photos developed by the time they return to the pub). Or go to a ceilidh (Scottish barn dance) – see www.ceilidh-club.com for details – they're on at least once a month in Camden or Battersea and they're a great laugh with a caller for beginners.

Clara

I love it. I ask a question. I get multiple responses. Cheers everyone, knew you wouldn't let me down. I now have several options for a Birthday bash. Perhaps I could combine elements of them all – roller disco involving a game of rounders with everyone dressed as Elvis followed by a Monopoly picnic on the ice rink...

Endless possibilities. I might change career and become a 'Random Events Birthday Celebration Organiser as Inspired by LbL' (REBCOILbL for short).

Ego sum mercator

ENGAGEMENT PARTIES

I recently got engaged and we are hoping to hold an engagement party soon – one which won't cost us a penny as we are both completely skint! London seems like the best option for everyone to be able to get to (on public transport so they can have a few beers), and we need to cater for a wide range of people, from families with kids through to mums, aunties and friends in their 20s and 30s. We're thinking of maybe asking a bar or restaurant to cordon off an area for us, maybe on a Saturday lunchtime so the family types can have food there? Then our mates our own age can join us later on to start some serious drinking and partying, and the family can go off and see some of the London sights... Anywhere in London would be good, but Covent Garden is particularly special because we first met there (in the *Porterhouse*!). Can anyone recommend any suitable *free* Saturday venues? Thanks guys.

gettingmarriedinthemorning

I'm getting married this year and had a similar dilemma –
want a nice place to celebrate that isn't going to break
the bank. I came up with the novel idea of trying wine
bars in The City and Docklands that are normally closed
at the weekends. I'm having my wedding reception in
Canary Wharf at *Corney & Barrow*. OK, not Covent
Garden but it's a very plush wine bar and I have
completely free hire. There is a minimum spend of
£2000 behind the bar which is easily enough done at
such occasions and they do jolly good food. Check out
www.corney-barrow.co.uk. Have a great party and
good luck with the wedding!

Jojo

Not sure if this will be of interest as not in Covent
Garden (but nearby), there is a pub on High Holborn –
Penderels Oak. It's a Wetherspoons, but they have a cellar
bar downstairs that they hire out for free, or they also
cordon off spaces in the large upstairs bar. The cellar bar
has music, and they do reasonably cheap food and drink
and are open till late. Have spent many an evening there
and had a great time!

fraggle

I'm not sure if it's free (we've managed to bargain them
down price-wise before now) but *The King's Arms* in
Roupell Street, Waterloo has a lovely back room and is

close to all local amenities (the *Station*, the *Eye*, *South Bank* etc.). Also, the *Blue Posts* in Newman Street, off Oxford Street, has an upstairs with its own bar. I know these two aren't particularly 'scenic', but they're well located. Hope it goes well!!!

Mamfer

WEDDING RECEPTIONS

Help! I'm getting married in Battersea in October and am yet to find a reception venue. I am looking for somewhere to do a sit-down meal for around 100 people then a disco. It needs to be not a million miles from Clapham Junction or ridiculously expensive – budget would probably stretch to £70 per head max. A hotel would be great as that'd give the family somewhere to stay, or else somewhere fairly central/near hotels etc. Does anyone have any original ideas?

claireabella

How about the following for ideas...

Winchester House in Putney – www.winchesterhouse. co.uk – contact is Terry Smith. They also have a licence for weddings. Lovely venue and very helpful.

Or *The Worx* – www.theworx.co.uk – venue is in Parsons Green. £2k or so should secure the 'Canteen' Area plus Studio 1 for dancing. Licence to 2 a.m. is possible. Come back to me if they try to charge you heaps of money.

The *White Horse* at Parsons Green has a large function room above the pub.

The *Warehouse Studio* – www.warehousestudio.co.uk – contact is Richard and it is in Earlsfield.

Not sure what will be going on with the *Marquee* in Battersea Park at that time of year... try contacting Alison Smith at Wandsworth Council.

Anyway. All the above are original. So best of luck.

Bo Tocks

The beautiful municipal halls at the back of BAC (*Battersea Arts Centre*), near Clapham Junction, are rented out for private hire and are popular for weddings. Try their website: www.bacvenues.org.uk/grand.htm.

Elin

I don't know if this appeals, but there's the *London Rowing Club* in Putney. Right on the river, big old balcony, reasonable rates for booze and food (wine starts around £10 a head and depending on the menu you

choose, food starts at around £18 a head). The room
rental costs £800–1000 depending on what you opt for,
and the other bits you organise yourself (though they
have contacts for DJs, decorating etc.). I'm getting
married there in a couple of weeks time (lah lah lah!)
and we've opted for a DIY experience but are really
looking forward to it. The man who organises events
there is really nice.

Monkeys Ahoy!

OK, there's this place – www.legothique.co.uk – that I
went to visit as a potential reception venue with my
bloke recently. Not too dear, kind of cool, amazing
building, and not actually that expensive as it goes. But
only you are allowed to go there, claireabella, and not
anyone else because I still want it to be relatively original
and not get booked up if we want to use it for next
year!

Bushbabyfish

I would thoroughly recommend the *Battersea Barge*:
www.batterseabarge.com. I nearly had my wedding
reception there (until I realised that I could make a killing
on selling my flat which meant we could spend loads of
dosh on the wedding). The owners are lovely, the
food's decent and they have a reasonable sound system.
Not sure exactly what their costs are these days but

they're not expensive, and not sure where the nearest hotel is, but there's probably a *Holiday Inn* or equivalent not that far away. Good luck with it all!

braindead geordie

PARTICULAR PLACES

BATTERSEA AT SUNDOWN

Any of you lovely LbLers know where I can get a decent sunset shot of *Battersea Power Station*? Willing to pay a bit of dosh for the right picture – it's a leaving present for a mate...

willster

Willster, have a look at www.flickr.com and enter 'Battersea power station' into the search box. Over 600 photographs will then be found. Decide on the one that you like the best and contact the photographer to arrange a print.

Eclectic Angel

There's often a stall at the Saturday market on Northcote Road in Clapham Junction which sells a variety of pictures of London. I seem to recall from experience that they have ones of *Battersea Power Station*, but they're all black and white so I don't know if they have any sunset ones – would sunset even show up on a black and white photo? Anyhoo – they have a lovely collection of photos of London landmarks.

Mel

How about going to *The Stationery Office* or *The Sorting Office* on Nine Elms Lane and asking them for access to one of the upper windows. If you get it right, you should have a beautiful shot looking due west. Alternatively, you could try contacting *Park View International* – www.parkview.co.uk – and ask them directly for access into the site. The security entrance is on Kirtling Street... just off Nine Elms Lane. Last option is to go and stand on Vauxhall Bridge and use a decent zoom lens.

Bo Tocks

OK, I'm not being cheeky here, I'm being completely genuine. Assuming you live in London yourself, why don't you get down there one of these evenings, while the weather's so nice, and take a photo yourself? Use a digital camera on the highest res possible – borrow a mate's if you don't have your own. Then spend the money instead on getting the photo professionally printed onto A3 photopaper, and buy a cheap frame. If that's too much money, you can find plenty of places on the net that will print your digital pic onto a mousemat (about a fiver) or a coffee-cup (about eight quid) if you shop around. It will be a lot more 'personal' and will mean much more as a gift if you bother to go and take the photo yourself. Even if you take crap photos, the gesture will mean much more, trust me.

Mestalla

A WOMAN'S PLACE

A while back (no idea how long) I read something (no idea what or where) about somebody (don't know who) who was setting up a trendy, young and cool Women's Institute type club in London. I have tried Googling it but I did not meet with much success. I think this is a cool idea, I would like to join! Does anyone anywhere have any idea what I may have read, if this club exists or where it is? Any info much appreciated. Thanks.

Maisy

Hey, I know about this – my girlfriend's involved.
They've done loads of great stuff, which has certainly
put paid to my brutal stereotyping! Here's a few details...
Fulham has a great WI which has been going for a
couple of years; they have done all sorts of exciting
things including appearing on Gordon Ramsay's *The 'F'
Word*. I've heard that they have just set a new WI up in
Covent Garden... and possibly more in the pipeline.
The new WIs have chocolate, beer and wine evenings,
salsa dancing, quad biking, environmental campaigns,
nutrition and fertility speakers, pole dancing, champagne
picnics and all sorts! New WIs in London have been set
up in the belief that the WI is a wonderful organisation
and it needs to be brought to a new, young generation of
women, here in the city. There is a host of campaigns to
be involved with that are fantastic. The local WIs can
provide great opportunities for friendship and fun as well
as bringing the community together. Joining a WI will
give women an opportunity to express their creativity,
take up new hobbies or just get two hours away from
their hectic life. Basically, if you feel particularly
adventurous you could set up a WI of your own; if
you can get a group of friends together in your area,
find somewhere to meet (the new ones meet in
pubs rather than village halls) and contact the WI,
they will help you set up. Check out the website:
www.womens-institute.org.uk.

Alternatively, you may like to join some of the WIs in
the London area, such as London West End, Fulham,

Jam Free (in Surrey) or others such as Covent Garden that are just starting out. For further information just contact the head office at membership@nfwi.org.uk.

Katie's Chap

The Fulham branch of the Women's Institute is mostly young women (20s/30s) and apparently lots of fun – I know a couple of girls who go regularly. Both are slightly jolly-hockeysticks sloaney head girl types but not at all prim and proper. Give it a go! www.fulhamwi.org.uk.

girl in pearls

BLUE POSTS

Can anyone tell me why there are three pubs called *The Blue Posts* within a short distance of one another.

Toomuchtimeonmyhands

I discovered many years ago that agreeing to meet friends in *The Blue Posts* in Soho would rarely result in success, hence quickly learned that there are four pubs called *The Blue Posts* (you've missed the one on Kingly Street). The posts apparently signified the four corners of the then hunting ground of Soho, when Soho, named after a hunting cry (rather like 'Tally-Ho'), was a small village on the outskirts of a London surrounded by fields.

Ads

Soho used to be Henry VIII's favourite hunting ground. *The Blue Posts* were literally that – blue posts upon which one could tie one's horse. Naturally, after parking one's horse after a busy day's huntin' a thirsty punter would need to slake his thirst with a pint of overpriced flat lager in a charmless Victorian retro-themed Georgian pub. They only had 300 years to wait.

Lovely Dai

FOOD AND DRINK

L ONDON IS... WINE BARS AND MOSTLY very expensive cocktails, mobile barmen and tight-fisted Jude Law exploiting the needy; London is jukeboxes and dining on rooftops, late-night coffee and early morning eggy bread; London is lardy cakes, oatcakes and liquorice; London is pie and mash. And liquor. Oh, and eels. London is eels...

Best breakfast ever?
'Eggs benedict at the Ivy as long as your rich godmother is paying.'

Poppy Tartt, food critic

ALCOHOL

MOBILE BARMEN

I'm organising a friend's hen do in London for early August. In between doing karaoke (her choice) and food, drinks will also be involved. She wants it to be a sophisticated affair and the other night I heard that there are mobile barman companies, that set up a bar and serve drinks wherever you are, outside. I was thinking it would be quite cool to do this in the *Italian Gardens* in Hyde Park or similar. There will be 12 of us – the only thing is that Googling brings up barmen for big massive dos and doesn't seem suitable for smaller ones (we aren't loaded!). Can anyone help?

Jolie Polly

I used this company for my thirtieth birthday last year and was very happy: www.brahmsandlizst.co.uk. From memory it cost £100 to hire them (including license) although I think there was a minimum spend too... Happy boozin'!

Glamazon

WINE BARS

Wine bars have a bit of a naff quality, thanks to the 1980s and 1990s, but surely there are still a lot of good ones around. Aren't there?

robram

One of the best used to be *Gordon's Wine Bar* on Villiers Street – all dank and atmospheric with mad bar staff, but it's gone off a little since a massive corporation moved its suited wage slaves in down the road. The *Grape Street Wine Bar* in Covent Garden is another gem – very friendly owner and a cracking list. And although it's in central Touristville, *Corks Wine Bar* in Leicester Square is surprisingly good.

Highbury Gal

Café des Amis (downstairs – it's a restaurant upstairs) on Hanover Place just off Long Acre in Covent Garden is a lovely little wine bar with great friendly staff. It's a little pricey but the wine is great and the food is amazing! They have recently starting serving spirits and bottled beers but people tend to stick to the wine. And a bonus is you get lots of poncy ballet and opera people in there!

wino

Gordon's Wine Bar next to Embankment tube is
excellent, especially on a summer's day when you can
make the most of the small garden. You're just about
more likely to get a seat there, than inside (its only
drawback is that it's too small).

Lucky

COCKTAILS

**Where can I taste London's best cocktails? And
although obviously, the main criteria here is taste,
price must also be taken into consideration. I can't
be paying £15 for a single glass of alcohol, no
matter how many bits of lime are in there. I just
can't do it. Not even a tenner really. For crying out
loud, I could get three bottles of wine for a tenner in
Tesco! But anyway, I do like cocktails. Anyone?**

Bo Jaxx

Freud. And that is all: www.london-drinking.com/
58.htm.

The Figurative Pineapple

Oh my god, Bo Jaxx, so many cocktail bars, so few hangover-free mornings... In no particular order, other than when I think of them:

The Player, Broadwick Street, W1

Bank, Aldwych, WC2

Detroit, Earlham Street, WC1

LoungeLover, Whitby Street, E1

Zebrano, Ganton Street, W1

Match, Clerkenwell Road, EC1

Don't think any of them are particularly cheap mind. I'm not sure cheap cocktails exist.

uberrich

I know what you mean about the extortionate prices charged by London bars for cocktails, especially as many of the places don't even include a whole measure of alcohol in them – just a lot of cheap made-from-concentrate orange juice and lemonade that comes out of that hand-held remote control lookey-like thing. I recently went to a bar off Drury Lane, though, called *Guanabara*, which is tucked away at the back of some theatre-looking thing. They make the best Brazilian cocktails in town and if you get there for happy hour you can enjoy the best Caipirinhas in town for just

£2.50. Yum, they are delicious! Check it out
www.guanabara.co.uk.

drinks-are-on-me

I'd recommend *B@1* (www.beatone.co.uk) – have been
to the ones in Richmond, Clapham Junction and
Covent Garden and they're always consistently brilliant.
Pretty sure their priciest on-menu cocktail is around £6,
and during happy hour it's two for one.

jp

If you've not been there you should definitely try *Jewel*.
I've only been to the *Jewel/Bar Blanca* (two bars, one
cocktail menu) on Piccadilly Circus but there's also a
new one on Maiden Lane near Covent Garden. The
cocktails were *gorgeous*, music funky and atmosphere
chilled. Drinks are under £7 (just!) and they certainly
used to do a two-for-one offer some afternoons. It's
slightly flouncy decor-wise but someone told me it's
owned by David Furnish so maybe that's no surprise!
Info at www.jewel-bar.co.uk.

Mine's a Melon Martini

The best cocktails in London, in fact in the whole world,
are at *Milk & Honey*, on Poland Street in Soho. Trust
me, I know my cocktails. £7 each, and worth every

penny. I recommend a Moscow Mule. They make their own ginger beer and it tastes fantastic, nothing like the alcopop. You need to book a table, and I think non-members have to leave at 11pm. The other reason I love *Milk & Honey* is the fact it's one of the few places in London with music quiet enough that you can have a conversation with mates without having to shout. I must be getting old... www.mlkhny.com.

Onil

This cocktails debate is bringing back dim memories of a cocktail bar in Soho which did excellent raspberry cocktails (I'm sure they did other things too). Unfortunately, we had such a good night, I can't remember what it was called or exactly where it was. Looking on the map, it was probably on Dean Street or Frith Street, on a corner. It was quite dark (I think) with wooden benches – nothing fancy or trendy about it, but excellent cocktails, and I don't remember them being expensive (although, apparently, I don't really remember much). It was great, so if anyone knows where I'm talking about, I'd like to find it again... Thank you all!

Ginja ninja

It was probably *LAB* on Old Compton Street, which does fantastic cocktails (try the Spear made with tequila

and black pepper – no really, it is fantastic, honest) and
has marvellously helpful staff, one of whom once helped
me into a frock which rather disastrously would not zip
up properly (note to self – eat fewer pies) and saved me
from having to go on a dinner date in my gym kit, bless
her kind heart. Music does get a bit loud later on
though.

pockettiger

Seconding the *Ruby Lounge* and their yummy cocktails.
The Driver (a little further up Caledonian Road, on the
corner of Wharfdale Road) is quite a nice pub too, with
excellent squashy sofas and chunky chips. For coffee,
panini, cake and so on, *Gran Sasso* (also on Cally Road)
is a fab little Italian cafe staffed by genuine charming
Italians. Oh, and there will soon be a *Starbucks* and a *Pret*
just by *McDonald's* outside the station. Hooray for
globalisation...

rosie posy

Check out *South London Pacific*, London's best tiki bar:
www.southlondonpacific.com.

Cocktails are under £4 till 10pm – their Trader Vic
Mai Tais are to die for. Gets more expensive if you're
planning on staying until three in the morning. I'll be
going there this weekend, as it happens. They have some

really fun nights as well, fun music, excellent tiki lounge stuff too. Wear Hawaiian shirts if possible.

Tris2000

COCKTAIL QUICKIES

LoungeLover, Shoreditch

cat

Henry J Beanz, Camden Town

Marga Rita

Detroit on Earlham Street, Covent Garden

moomintroll

Thirst, Greek Street

cybermunkee

Zakudia, near Southwark Bridge

wicked witch of the west end

As a gnat's chuff

I was at a party a couple of weeks ago, at an all-night London dodgy drinking den, and I bought Judo Law a whisky and coke which set me back £7 (being a screenwriter I wanted to do some networking). He was pleasant for two minutes then completely blanked me mid conversation. Half an hour later I bumped into him again and asked him if he wanted a drink, he did (another £7) and was pleasant to me for about two minutes then blanked me once more. A while later we were both at the bar – by now it was about five in the morning – waiting to be served. He acknowledged me and nodded; I waited for him to offer to buy me a drink back. He didn't so I thought I'd jog his memory. 'Can I get you a drink, Jude?' expecting him to say, 'Oh, no, it's my round.' But he said, 'Yes, can I have a double single-malt whisky and coke, and a still mineral water'. That would have cost me £18. I'm unemployed too. I was furious. But while he wasn't looking I bought him a single house whisky and coke, a glass of tap water, and before giving him the drinks I licked both straws. And I had a terrible cold at the time. I didn't bother even trying to make conversation with him, just handed him the drinks and went to talk to some make-up artists instead. Tight cunt.

Tris2000

LONDON'S BEST PUBS

Who's for creating the best London pub list ever? I'll start:

Best tucked away pub: *Lamb and Flag*, Lamb's Conduit Street

Best pub in Soho: *The Endurance*, Berwick Street

Best pub on the river: *The Dove*, Hammersmith

Best pub in a London village green: *The Sun Inn*, Barnes

Best pub to pretend you're in a Shakespeare play: *George Inn*, Borough.

Mine's a pint

Best Bloody Mary: *Sun and Doves*, Camberwell

Best Pint of Guinness: *Retro Bar*, Strand

Best Pub Garden: *The Flask*, Highgate

Best River Pub: *The Mayflower*, Rotherhithe

And another: *Captain Kidd*, Wapping.

Woodenhorse

Best Pub for Big Screen Football: *The Famous 3 Kings*, West Kensington

Best Pub Quiz: *The Royal Inn on the Park*, Lauriston Road/Victoria Park Road (Tuesdays)

Best Gay Pub: *The Retro Bar*, George Court (excellent for Eurovision Parties, second Thursday of every month)

Best Pub for Late Night Knees-up: *The Palm Tree*, Haverfield Road, E3

Best Pub for Banging Your Head: *Ye Olde Cheshire Cheese*, Fleet Street

Best Pub for Jukebox: *Bradley's Spanish Bar* (upstairs), Hanway Street (plays six-inch singles!)

Best Pub for Late Night Beer Garden: *The Duke of Edinburgh*, Ferndale Road, Brixton

Best Pub for Swedish Cider: *Harcourt Arms*, Harcourt Road W1H

Best Pub to Have a Quirky Tradition: *The Widow's Son*, Devons Road (watch a sailor stick a hot cross bun on the ceiling of the pub every Good Friday since the mid 1800s)

Best (read only) Pub to Buy Stamps: *The Mayflower*, Rotherhithe Street (UK and US stamps!)

Worst Pub for Terrible Toilets: *St Christopher's Inn*, Borough

Worst Pub for Completely Wrecking a Perfectly Decent Boozer Because of Overzealous Refurbishment/ Revamping: *Dusk*, Battersea Park Road (previously a wonderful boozer called *The Legless Ladder*, which turned into *G2* and now a pseudo-trendy bar called *Dusk*).

Tris2000

Best pub for standing at the bar so long that you get fed up and go to the offy by the station instead and are outside by the river having a beer before your mate gets served: *The Hornimans*, London Bridge.

Bad books – *The North Star, Ealing*

Pubs: if you are serving last orders till 11pm, it's reasonable to assume that those punters haven't downed their drinks – like someone suffering from extreme dehydration – by 11.03pm. It's also a pretty safe bet that if you send round, not bar staff, but hired goons demanding everyone vacate the place, every 38 seconds from thereon, you're not going to be met with agreeable smiles and polite compliance. You're probably going to get people's backs up. Another key to success would be not to beat the living shit out of blokes who, okay, are getting a bit lary, but essentially are just asking for five minutes to drink up, get their coats on and get the fuck home. So, my question to The North Star *in Ealing is 'do you feel lucky?' When the bar staff battened down the hatches on Saturday night, and the goons came in and delivered some sort of death-match violence on three harmless lads, did I capture the 'Prince Naseem wannabe' reigning blows*

*and kicks to the guy on the floor on my trusty Nokia
6630? Did I get all the faces of the bouncers, not
restraining, but kicking the crap out these guys? Well
did I, punks?*

Hairy Leper

JUKEBOX

**Where can I find decent jukebox pubs in London,
these days? They're as rare as England rugby
victories!**

Zabadak

Try *The Reliance Bar* (333, Old Street). Their jukebox is
pretty good and it is an OK bar too.

Music lover

I highly recommend *The Warwick* on Essex Road, *The
Endurance* in Soho and *Bradleys* on Hanway Street for
their music selections. And they have the added bonus

of being top places to have a swift half or three. The
Boogaloo has a good jukebox too but the choice of
records does scream 'pretentious indie know-it-all'.

rumlovesme

The *Social* on Little Portland Street, W1 is also
outstanding.

Randy Alexander

The Green on Clerkenwell Green has a free jukebox. The
stuff on it is pretty obvious – Bowie, Blondie, Van
Morrison etc. – but since you don't have to put any
pennies on the slot you can't really go wrong.

The Assassin Prince

CIDER AND PIES

**Please god someone help me! It's fast approaching
that time of year I should be getting myself worked
up into a frenzy of excitement for the eventual arrival
of the Glastonbury festival, but as some of you are
probably aware, it's not on this year (sob, sob).
Anyhow, what I'm trying to do is recreate some
of that vibe here in London (sans mud) and I'm
desperate to find a pub, market, offy etc., that serves**

up the finest pint of (a) boiling hot spicy cider a la
Cider bus, and/or (b) Brothers Pear Cider (perry for
you purists out there). I've been searching for the
last year to no avail! There must surely be a pub/
hangout for you West Country types here in the
big smoke? In exchange for this info I will supply
the location of the excellent PieMeister, who
single-handedly kept me alive last year from their
stall next to the dance tent... they have a stall in
Borough Market, yay! (If you have one of their pies
you will know how valuable this info is!)

Partyboy

I'm not sure if these places are up to Glastonbury
standards, Partyboy, but my cider-drinking friend
recommends the *Priory Arms* for Thatchers cider or
Chimes in Pimlico for all kinds of cider. As for pies, the
Vibe bar on Brick Lane has just started selling Pieminister
pies. For someone who doesn't really like pies or cider I
seem to know a worrying amount...

Zogs

Partyboy, I do believe the Scandinavian bar *Nordic* on
Newman Street in W1 serves Pear Cider. The reason I
know this is because a friend was insistent I try some
recently as it was apparently delicious, but sadly, after
one too many hot ciders last year at Glasto, and the

particularly unfortunate effect it had on me (face down on the grass, very sick, missing three main acts on the Pyramid Stage and *all* of my dignity as a result) I couldn't so much as sniff the bottle. Anyway, enjoy!

 NikNaks

The *Defectors Weld* in Shepherd's Bush (170 Uxbridge Road, W12 8AA) sells Brothers Pear Cider!! I was very excited to find this out when visiting the pub for the first time before a recent gig at the *Shepherd's Bush Empire*. The pub is owned by the same people that own the *Lock Tavern* in Camden, so it's possible it's sold there as well!

 MarkyG

They do do it at the *Lock Tavern* in Camden and you can get it delivered to your house, so you can sit in your garden in the summer. I'd recommend this cider to everyone, it can't be beaten. Also on the cider thing, I'd recommend the *Duke of Cambridge* in Angel, which does some amazing Devon Scrumpy on tap that always reminds me of *Glastonbury Cider Bus*.

Enjoy cider!

 rowdybeans

In response to Partyboy's plaintive quest, I can impart the following info:

1. Cider – Borough Market is the best I've found. There's a stall just near the restaurant *Fish* that does the best hot spiced cider I've had this side of the *Cider Bus* at Glasto, and even better, they'll provide flagons of cider and little bags of cider spice so you can recreate at home.
2. Pear Cider – only pub I've ever seen Brothers Bar pear cider in is the *Defectors Weld* on Shepherd's Bush Green. They were selling bottles just after I returned from Glasto last year. Don't know if they still sell it, but worth a try.

corporatescum

If you want a pub/hangout for West Country people try the *Cove Bar* on 1 The Market, The Piazza, Covent Garden which is owned by the *West Cornwall Pasty Company* and is supposed to look like a Cornish tin mine (which apparently is a good thing); it's the only pub I know in London where you climb up two floors and feel like you're deep underground. Anyway, if you want to buy some Pear Cider to take away, then why not go to your nearest *Wetherspoons* pub and buy one of their bottles of perry to take home with you? But your best option might be to go to the *London Drinker Beer and Cider Festival*, go up to the

Cider Bar and talk face to face with the experienced barstaff there who have deep, personal knowledge of every cider and perry outlet in London. There'll probably be a bearded hobbit there called Simon who is especially knowledgeable (have a look at www.camranorthlondon.org.uk for more info).

Cheers!

Eclectic Angel

You will be delighted – nay thrilled and overjoyed as believe me we were – to discover that Brothers are now DELIVERING – yes right to YOUR DOOR... the most lovely loveliest pear cider of Glastonbury fame. You can get more info here www.brotherscider.co.uk. We have ordered cases a couple of times since last year for pre-Christmas and New Year parties. It's not the same as drinking it in a field with 120,000 other people, but it's a close second... ENJOY!!! (And if you other LbLrs have no idea what we are talking about then I would highly recommend just ordering a case just for the hell of it – yes it's expensive – but it's lovely and it gets you pissed really quickly so you don't need that much of it.)

Katey K

Healthy

SHOP

Does anyone know where I can find a really decent health food shop. Must have mountainous quantities of dirty vegetables, 'barley cup', a kaleidoscopic array of tofu, staff that wear patchwork 'festival trousers' and a table covered in petitions for various radical organisations... You know the sort of place I mean. Ideally, everyone in there should smell of dope and sandalwood. I myself am not of a particularly crusty persuasion but I'm a veggie and I have a burning need to buy nut loaves and pulses in huge unmarked bags, and to rub filthy shoulders with eco-brethren. I live in West Dulwich and I work in South Ken, but I'm happy to travel high and low for the crustiest of treats.

Samuel K.

Well Samuel, have you tried *Fresh and Wild*? The ones in Camden and in Soho are huge and satisfyingly full of barley and dirty vegetables. There is also a great health food shop in *Greenwich Market* which doesn't sell veggies but just about all else is covered pulse-wise. You could also wait until next year when *Wholefoods Market* open their new store in the old *Barkers* building at High Street

Kensington. See: www.wholefoods.com for more info.
Happy Mung Beaning!

parsnipsatdawn

HEALTH SHOP QUICKIES

Mother Earth **on Albion Road, Stoke Newington**

PopC

Brixton Wholefoods **on Atlantic Road, Brixton**

robram

VEGIVORES

It can be difficult to find a really great restaurant for a special occasion couple night-out where one is vegetarian and the other is not. Any suggestions?

thepathologist

Yeah – how about any great vegetarian restaurant!? Not to be a complete smart-arse, but great vegetarian food is great food. And, while I can sort of understand how people decide not to be vegetarian, I'm unable to understand how anyone could not manage to be vegetarian *for one meal*. Okay, please pardon my unseemly outburst. Check the listings at: www. happycow.net/europe/england/london.

For an upscale nice night out, I'd recommend the *Gate*: www.thegate.tv – described by the *City Secrets: London* guide as 'one of the most magical courtyards and best vegetarian restaurants in London. Set behind a beautiful iron gate in a tranquil leafy courtyard... a light-filled restaurant with deep yellow painted walls... candlelit evening meal.' Oh, and *alright* – if one of the couple *insists* on having seared flesh available, then try any great Thai, Indian, Korean, Ethiopian or Vietnamese joint. All of those cuisines are (generally, depending on the particular restaurant) extremely veg-friendly. Good luck.

 Mr Fuches

There is an extremely super dooper veggie restaurant near the Barbican called *Carnevale*. It's a deli during the day and in the evening it turns into a restaurant. If you go there you must ask for the room out the back, which is a little conservatory with a glass roof and lots of plants. The food is great – the wine is veggie, they have forced rhubarb for pudding, and they ain't expensive. Even I enjoyed it and I love a good bit of well hung meat.

 *Meat and two veg*

The *Blue Elephant* near Fulham Broadway tube is an excellent Thai restaurant for special occasions – they have separate veggie and meat and fish eater menus, so the veggies feel well looked after. The food and service is good, the atmosphere excellent. Expect to pay £40–50 a head though...

Prawn

Morgan M's in Islington is a very classy French restaurant with both normal meat menu and a full veggie menu. The concentrated beetroot puree is to die for. I'd also recommend *Axis* at One Aldwych, a great dramatic dining room with decent veggie options. Of the properly vegetarian restaurants, *Mildred's* in Soho is great value and not too terrifying for carnivores.

NotQuiteVeggie

I can sympathise, having been the veggie other half of a meat lover for several years. *Chez Bruce* over in Wandsworth will always give you a couple of lovely veggie options if you warn them when you book, and the same goes for *River Cafe* (although it'd have to be a *really* special occasion as their pricing policy is a little insane – although on the plus side the veg options are much cheaper!). *The Bleeding Heart* is also worth a go, or go for tapas – *Navarro's* and *Fino's* (both in the West End) are great, and there's a huge veggie selection to choose from. Incidentally, my meat-loving other half deserted me for a fellow meat-eater earlier this year, so anyone who'd like to take his place as the provider of expensive meals across London, do let me know – I can only afford to eat in *McDonald's* at the moment, not the ideal place to practise a veggie lifestyle!

Special K

The best veggie restaurant that I have been to as a non-veggie girlfriend of a veggie is *Eat and Two Veg* on Marylebone High Street – www.eatandtwoveg.com – And it's a good place for star-spotting too!

xforxray

NUTROAST

My sister is vegetarian and every Christmas we spend hours trying to make her something that resembles a 'special' Christmas dinner. Can anyone suggest where I might actually go and buy some kind of replacement meat dish that she can have with her potatoes and sprouts?

Eve

My veggie boyfriend and I often have Cauldron Foods' Mushroom Bake as a Sunday lunch – very yummy and easy. Making your own nut roast from scratch is one of

the most god-forsaken tasks in the vegetarian cook's
repertoire and *not* to be recommended.

Cassius

Why do you need a 'replacement meat' substitute? As a
veggie for health reasons and not animal rights I actually
don't like the meat replacement products. Why not
cook your sister something like a savoury pancake filled
with spinach, blue cheese and walnuts? Not too tricky to
cook, a bit different and very very tasty. Mmmmmmm.

Veggie 4 Health

Why don't you suggest to your sister that she cooks her
fucking pointless miserable veggie meal herself instead of
making you slave away in the kitchen for hours? Then
she might realise how incredibly annoying and selfish it
is to make people who are not veggies cook for veggies
when they have better things to do. Like eating turkey.

Boney M

Hey, Boney M, calm down a bit. Have you got a bit
hyper on all the chemicals in meat these days? Eve
probably wants to do something special for her sister
because she cares about her and there are plenty of dishes
you can buy in health food shops and supermarkets (I
even saw Tesco advertising a nut and cranberry roast).
And anyway, who's being annoying and selfish? Perhaps

you should educate yourself with some facts before
accusing others of selfishness:

- Meat eaters contribute to global warming. There are
  two man-made things that can be seen from space –
  the *Great Wall of China* and the burning of the
  Amazonian rain forests to breed cattle for the meat
  industry
- It takes about 10 kg of good-quality plant protein
  such as wheat and soya fed to animals to produce 1kg
  of meat. How about using that plant food to feed
  starving people instead?
- 90% of the UK's animal feed protein concentrates
  come from poor countries – often those where
  children die from starvation
- 40 million tonnes of grain is needed to end world
  hunger; 540 million tonnes of grain is fed to animals
  in the West (info from United Nations)
- Meat eaters are more of a burden on the NHS.
  Vegetarians have lower rates of obesity, coronary
  heart disease, high blood pressure, large bowel
  disorders, cancers and gallstones (info from British
  Medical Association)
- Meat eaters are being unkind to their body – meat is
  high in fat and cholesterol and has no carbohydrates.
  The vegetable products that they feed to the animals
  that are killed for meat contain protein, vitamins,
  minerals, fibre and are low in fat. What a bizarre way
  of doing things.

It's your choice to contribute to global warming, the starving millions and your own ill health. And you do it because you enjoy eating meat. But please stop to think before you next accuse someone of being selfish.

So tuck into your turkey and enjoy it but try and raise a smile! It is nearly Christmas.

Veggie 4 Health

Veggie 4 Health and Eve – my humblest apologies. When I re-read my reply I was shocked at my over-reaction to a simple harmless question. My only defence was having just cooked a meal for five veggies, one who doesn't like fish, one who doesn't eat any meat, one who eats some organic meat, one who doesn't eat anything apparently and one who doesn't like my cooking. Suffice to say, a weekend was wasted trying to be inventive with vegetables and cooking all sorts of different versions of things to please everyone and no one ate any of it then proceeded to complain. All I knew, in my crazed state, was that I am the perfect guest, I eat everything, am easy to cook for and grateful for anything someone cooks for me. Phew. Anyway – my apologies again. I was being irrational. Must have been the onset of bird flu.

Boney M

It's a big fat lie that you can see the *Great Wall of China* from space. I was on the *wall* in October and although it may be extremely long it's only about three metres wide. That would be like seeing a country road from space. I wonder how many of your other facts are urban myths too.

Bored

Interesting to read about meat eaters contributing to global warming... Do you know that cows themselves are considered to contribute directly owing to the amount of methane produced by herds of grazing cattle? I guess it should help to minimise long-term effects if we all ate more beef...

ilikecows

Damn left-wing liberal hippie vegetarian propaganda. Seriously though, most of the points Veggie 4 Health has stated are false or misconstrued. Created by vegetarians to make them feel better about themselves and to try and make meat eaters feel like the scum of the earth. I could sit here and refute every one of your points, but what use would that do? You would still look down your nose upon us meat eaters with disdain. How about we all get along? My girlfriend is a veggie, yet she has no qualms with me eating meat. How about everyone eat or do what they like, as long as it ain't hurting or harming others. They way I see it, eating meat hasn't hurt anyone but the eaten. Let's eat what we want to eat without

having a sermon about it. Geez, you'd think veggie/
vegan is some sort of new religion with the amount of
effort people go into to try and convert meat eaters.

dalore

NOT BISCUITS

**We've had a few questions recently about foreign
foodstuffs (biltong etc.) which made me wonder.
Somewhere in London must stock Staffordshire
Oatcakes – if you think I'm asking about biscuits
you needn't reply. Ooh, and is it still not possible to
get a proper Bakewell Pudding outside Bakewell?
I'm a Londoner by birth but I've been feeling
homesick lately for the land of my fathers (or
mother).**

dwp

If you mean the ones that you have at brekky that you
put egg, sausage and bacon into and roll up then I
believe that you can get them at any LARGE *Sainsbury's*,
don't think the smaller *Sainsbury's* stock them.

Rusky

You can get Staffordshire Oatcakes (not biscuits!) at *Neal's Yard Dairy*. They certainly have them in their Borough branch (6 Park Street, SE1 9AB), so presumably they stock them in the Covent Garden one (17 Shorts Gardens, WC2H 9UP) too.

Caro

The *North Staffs Oatcakes* website (www.nsoatcakes.co.uk) lists *Neal's Yard Dairy* as a stockist, but I haven't been to see for myself. I'm about to put in an order via their website. From my quick research on this not so long ago, they seem to be the cheapest. Enjoy!

strawberryfluff

I sympathise with your search for Staffordshire Oatcakes and Bakewell Puddings – I have still to find a proper Bakewell Pudding anywhere – but you can buy Staffordshire Oatcakes from *Tesco Extra* and larger stores, i.e. the one at Colney Hatch lane. Enjoy!!

Curly

I'm afraid that you can only get Bakewell Puddings from the *Bakewell Pudding Shop* in, funnily enough, the town of Bakewell! For the masses this is not to be confused with the Bakewell Tart – a Mr Kipling rip-off and not abuse towards the young ladies of the area. Have you tried a Derbyshire Oatcake?

eternally northern

LIQUORICE SOLUTION

I have chosen (so my girlfriend tells me) to give up smoking. I'm not sure I believe the hype about 'replacement products' given the short time it takes to get over the physical addiction. What really helped last time (I know I know) was  **some of the really, really, really 'Bruce Lee' hard liquorice that came in six-inch sticks with a stamped bit at the end. I think it was Barretts or summat. Anyone seen it recently? I could do with a crate-load to get through pub scenarios and still have lovely yellow teeth. I thank you.**

fractious

Being a fellow liquorice lover I know (and love) the hard sticks you mean – unfortunately I have not seen them for years, but I used to buy them for 5p at *The Candybox* in 1978. Eek. This website is good though for lots of different sorts of my fave sweet: www.valentines-liquorice.co.uk. Good luck with the giving up smoking. Hope you make it.

Liquoricegirl

Hey, fractious, try this website: www.aquarterof.co.uk. A great great site which surprisingly has a vast array of all the old sweets we all loved as kids! Parma violet anyone? Kola Kubes?

Sherbert dip

Hey, fractious, I can't help you with the liquorice but my girlfriend has also decided that I want to give up smoking. The problem is, although I know I should, I really don't want to (yet). Does anyone know of a cunning way of getting partners to drop the subject? Alternatively, I am considering sticking nicotine patches on her when she sleeps so I can get her hooked on the evil weed too, then we can both puff away in perfect harmony. Any other suggestions?

bored

UNHEALTHY

LARDY CAKES

I may be cursed for this, but I'm not a born-and-bred Londoner and I'm very happy that I'm not. You see, I was born and raised in the most wonderful city in the land – Southampton. When you've stopped laughing I'll explain why Southampton will forever be superior to London. No, it doesn't have the London atmosphere, the London pubs and bars, the London restaurants, the London theatres or the London galleries. And yet, it's still superior for one reason: Lardy Cakes. You can buy Lardy Cakes in Southampton. You can't in London. Can any of you proud Londoners put up a defence of London, change my mind, and tell me where I can buy a big, sticky, coronary-inducing Lardy Cake in London? Convert me. Convert me to your city.

Torres

This just makes me like London more. Cakes made out of lard???

come off it

At last something to rival the great metropolis; across the capital you can find 24-hour falafel and sushi but no lardy cake. It would make a delightful high cholesterol alternative to the battery chicken and chips in an orange box favoured across London but without the cruelty and litter. But no I wouldn't move back to Southampton for a lifetime's free supply either...

Big T

Southampton is an absolute hole, full of vile sub-Corbusier architecture and hair-gelled semiliterate knobheads out on the beer. The SINGLE and ONLY THING it has over London is that it is slightly less far on the train to Swanage. As for lardy cakes, I think you just made that up as I've never seen one here or even heard of someone else knowing someone who once ate a bit of one.

MovingFromSouthamptonToLondonVerySoon

PIE AND MASH

I'm looking for a really good, authentic East End pie and mash cafe. I have stumbled across a couple in Bethnal Green – *G Kelly* and *S and R Kelly*. Has anyone ever been to either? If so, what did you think? Does anyone have any other recommendations? Thanks a million!

Missred

Try *L Manzes* along Walthamstow market: tiled walls, big counter, bowls filled with dubious liquor and eels. Then buy some of the best and cheapest veg in town from the market stalls, wondering to yourself why *Sainsbury's* charges so much for so little...

Monkeys Ahoy

Whatever happened to proper English grub? And not those awful *Wetherspoons* imitations either. Well I found it – the best pie and mash I ever had and for only £2 with gravy or liquor in Greenwich *Cutty Sark*! It's called *Goddard's* pies and you'll never want to waste £2 on *Pret-a-bloody-Manger* again!

just_give_me_some_credit

Manzes – www.manze.co.uk – it is fabulous. Proper meat (of undetermined nature) pies, mash scraped onto the side of your plate and lovely green liquor. Eels as well if they float your boat, and wash it all down with a mug of hot sarsparilla. All served by grumpy old women in dinner lady outfits. Perfect reminder of childhood Saturday lunches with my Nan. Oh yummy, I am starving now.

TK

By 'East End' I'm not sure if you're looking for a pie and mash shop just in the East End area or whether you just want a traditional East End-style shop. Either way, I'm going to recommend *Manzes* either on Tower Bridge Road (10-minute walk from Borough tube) or Peckham High Street. Both still have the old tiled interior with long wooden bench seating, coupled with gorgeous pies and, er, mash. The liquor they serve is the best in London I think. I was disappointed with *Goddard's* in Greenwich – bit more tourist-oriented and the food just isn't as tasty. Although a terrible name, *Cockneys Pie and Mash* on Portobello Road is surprisingly good, but it's a fairly recent addition and it's not particularly conventional in decor. Other than that, *Cookes* on Goldhawk Road is well worth a visit, as is *Castle's* by Camden Road station. An old childhood hangout of mine was *Arments*, off the Walworth Road – probably my favourite for this reason alone but the food is also very good and it's one of the cheapest around. *R Cooke* on The Cut near Waterloo was good too but that shut down and there's a Chinese restaurant there instead... as I found out much to my distress last year.

Two and two

Pig pond
Can anyone tell me the name of the picture of the pig jumping into a pond which hangs in the **Hamburger Union** *on Dean Street, Soho? Thank you!*

Bert

It's painted by a German chap called Michael Sowa and is called Kohler's Schwein, *which is German for something. You can buy greetings cards with that and other paintings by him in the shops.*

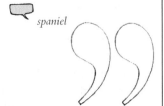
spaniel

WRY FRY UP

Does anyone have any recommendations for places to go and have an excellent or weird or decadent or humorous breakfast. I edit the *London Review of Breakfasts* and am always looking for ideas.

Malcolm Eggs

Papa Del's opposite Highgate station at the top of Archway Road does a wicked breakfast at the weekend. Full English, Italian style (Italian sausage, Italian meats instead of bacon etc.).

Hobbes

The Villandry on Great Portland Street do a lovely breakfast. Open nice and early which is perfect if you want a nice before-work-catch-up with a friend. I also remember reading an interview with Danni Minogue where she said Kylie has a breakfast at *Tiffany's* for friends where everything came draped in diamonds!

pankcakes and maple syrup (ok bacon as well)

Get yourself to *Maggie's* in Lewisham – it's the best fry-up south of the river. Eat as much sausage, egg, hash brown, bacon, beans, tomato, chips, onion rings (yes, onion rings), mushrooms and the like for a fiver and Maggie even makes an appearance to refill your tea!

Chunkalunka

What about the pubs which open early, e.g. in Smithfield? I occasionally used to meet friends for a pint at about 8 a.m., then toddle into work!

Zabadak

For the best in old school Italian caffs, you cannot beat *Pellicci's* on Bethnal Green Road. It's a dollhouse-sized emporium of wood, frothy coffee, formica and family-run fun. Generations of Pellicci's will make you welcome alongside the regulars which are a mix of East End market-stall traders, arty/TV types, and people who 'resemble' henchmen of the Krays.

pippylongstocking

With your name you'd appreciate the vegan breakfast here then: www.eatandtwoveg.com. They also do non-vegan breakfasts, if you're that way inclined...

Angel

I had a humorous encounter at *Rock Steady Eddie's* in Camberwell Green about a year ago. After a late night partying, those who had slept over at my boyfriend's place all woke up at 11ish and headed out to the nearest café. *Rock Steady Eddie's* is, strangely, owned by a chap called Eddie who often dresses up as Elvis. He also has a Karaoke machine set up and can be heard singing the old tunes from time to time This particular morning when we got there and ordered breakfast, my boyfriend made up this story and told Eddie that it was my birthday. That was it, Eddie (quite a tall guy) whisked me up the aisles of the cafe whilst singing 'Are You Lonesome Tonight' to music which he put on his Karaoke machine!! And later, after

I had eaten my breakfast, he brought me a dollop of ice cream with two lit matchsticks singing happy birthday!

LonesomeGirl

Though the food isn't weird or wacky but just a really good honest fry-up everyone should go to the *New Piccadilly Café* on Denman Street off Shaftesbury Avenue. It's a '50s style cafe (in the sense that the place is literally the same as it was in the '50s) with a good dollop of character and is cheap as chips (primary reason that it might not be there for very much longer since the rents round there are obviously sky-high). An endangered species by all accounts; catch it while you can.

Cafe lover

FOREIGN FOOD

OKONOMI-YAKI

Have recently returned from Japan (it was amazing, thanks for asking!) and while I was there had the best meal I've had in a long time... okonomi-yaki. Now I'm desperate to find somewhere in London where I can eat this again... Have found one place but they won't let you cook it yourself which is half the fun. Any ideas?

unsurewotshappening

Abeno Okonomi-Yaki in Museum Street. You'll need to book though – it gets busy.

Anon

Abeno and *Abeno Too* (in WC1 and WC2, respectively) are both okonomi-yaki. I doubt they'll let you cook the meal yourself, though. Good food, by the way – I've eaten in both.

dawnage

JAPANESE

In keeping with the Japanese theme poem in last week's LbL newsletter, I asked a Jap-obsessed friend of mine where to eat out the other night and here are her recommendations. *Satsuma* on Wardour Street is like *Wagamama* but the food is more authentic. For conveyor belt sushi, recommend *Kulukulu Sushi* on Brewer Street. *Ten ten tei* on Brewer street is also good, for fairly cheap homely Japanese cooking – I recommend the katsu curry bento! *Ikkyu* on Tottenham Court Road is good for getting lots of bits and pieces to share. Share and you shall find.

Dave

I'm glad my Haiku inspired you to seek out Japanese food, Dave – it's a topic I'm always happy to read about! Though I'm not Japanese I do know what my stomach likes, and I can back up your friend's recommendations (especially about the sushi at *Kulukulu* – went there last week for the first time in long while, and I'm still fantasising about the size and freshness of their tuna). On the topic of Japanese food, I have a question: can anyone recommend a good ramen place? The best I've been able to find in London has been at *Sakura*, but their standards fluctuate. I've tried many places, so I'd be interested to hear what other people's experiences are in the search for a good bowl of noodles.

Haiku Annie

Dave, thanks very much for the tips. In the spirit of sharing I will divulge away. One of the best sushi places in London is *Sushi Hiro* on Uxbridge Road opposite Ealing Common tube. There is a big Japanese population in Ealing because of the nearby Japanese school; the chef at *Hiro* allegedly quit *Nobu* to ascend to a higher plane in some sort of sushi purification ritual. Inside, it is like being in Kyoto, all white and sparse, sushi-only, mostly Japanese patrons – a gem.

rachel-san

Thanks Dave! I have a Japanese housemate who's missing sushi like crazy. Her first reaction to the whale/Thames spectacle was to ask if we were going to eat it. Can I also recommend *Sakura* on Hanover Square? I can? Oh, thanks. It's really good. Try the shochu, weirdest booze I've ever drunk.

spaniel

FRENCH TOAST

My hubby is a huge fan of French toast (American style). Anyone know where we can get great big slabs of it (preferably made with challah bread) with maple syrup? Thanks in advance.

M

French Toast American style? Surely you are joking? French Toast by definition is what it is... what you want is some bastardised version that you'll only find by making it in your own kitchen!! Just be thankful this wasn't posted in *ParisbyParis* or you'd have an angry mob banging down your door, screaming about the protection of the French culture and cuisine from the English-speaking world.

Cubikrube

I personally prefer American Toast (French style). But each to their own.

Bored

French toast? FRENCH toast??? Now, is it me or does that name sound far too glamorous for what French toast actually is? I spent two years living in France and never uncovered the mystery of what it actually was... until I met some Californians who made it for me for breakfast one day. Was I excited? Very. Couldn't wait to see what this mythical breakfast goodness would look and taste like... I expected sweet piles of French cuisine goodness crammed onto a beautiful plate covered in an exotic sauce of some nature... And then I was presented with... EGGY BREAD!!! Unbelievable. I really wouldn't bother traipsing across London to find a cafe that sells it. Come to my house. I'll do it for free, with free-range eggs, ketchup and all. So there. French toast? Harrumph...

Gem

Hoxton Bar and Kitchen (on Hoxton Square) do some mighty fine French Toast with maple syrup, sour cream, and fruit compote of a weekend. They do an impressive pancake stack too with bacon and maple syrup. Top hangover food!

Michael

SPECIAL OCCASION FOOD

XMAS LUNCH

The Boss has just sprung on me to book us somewhere nice for an Xmas lunch – preferably somewhere not too far from the South Bank. Not a large group but suddenly bereft of ideas... Probably on the piss afterwards, so could do with being local to pleasing bars...

Velma

I've just come back from a lovely liquidy lunch session at *The Garrison* on Bermondsey Street. More info at: www.thegarrison.co.uk.

I work on the South Bank myself, and it takes about 10 to 15 minutes in a cab to get there. Food is good, service friendly, and the atmosphere is very cosy and relaxed. In short, recommended.

karal88

You could do worse than try Borough High Street. Have Xmas lunch at the *George* (*George Inn Yard*), a

gorgeous old 1600s galleried pub. After that, walk south
in the direction of Borough, ending at the *Dover Castle*
(6a Great Dover Street) which is open all night and is
free to get in (and cheap prices). If you get too pissed
you can even stay the night there – £10 and they throw
in breakfast and a sauna, and you don't need to be a
youth hostel member!)

Tris2000

There is the Greek souvlaki place – not that festive but
great views – on the South Bank there is *Bankside* on
Southwark Bridge Road – more festive, good food, not
too pricey there is *GeorgeTown* – a bit random but fun –
it's the restaurant in the *London Bridge Hotel* that does
Malaysian/Indo type food and has a man tinkling away
on the piano while you eat. Looks quite posh but not
expensive and feels as though you are treating
yourselves. Bet they have a Christmas menu.

Polly

DAD

**At the beginning of December it's Dad's sixtieth
birthday so to mark the occasion the family's
planning a day trip to the Big Smoke for a bit of
sight-seeing and to watch *High Society* (Dad's a big**

Cole Porter fan). Anyway, please could someone recommend a good restaurant on or near Shaftesbury Avenue that isn't a tourist trap and isn't too young person and trendy; it is his sixtieth after all! Thanks.

Oracle

Could I recommend the *Italian Kitchen*? Just up the road – very friendly and welcoming. I think the food is great and the pre-theatre menu is always good too (especially the soups). One word of warning – the bread is far too delicious; don't eat too much as the servings are very generous...

pockettiger

There's a fantastic vegetarian, South Indian restaurant called *Woodlands* on Panton Street, meaning it's ideal for pre-theatre dinner. The food's divine and my dad, who very much feels that dinners are better if they have meat in them, loved it there.

Hannah

Why not take your Dad for an old-fashioned Soho experience at *Kettners*? It's just off Shaftesbury Avenue. Don't be put off by the fact it's called a Champagne Bar

– it's atmospheric without being too loud and special enough for a birthday dinner: www.kettners.com.

Highbury Gal

Bali Bali on Shaftsbury Avenue is an *amazing* Indonesian/ Thai/Malaysian restaurant, if you like that kind of food. The dishes are some of the most authentic Asian dishes I have experienced in London and the staff are very friendly. It's a short walk east of Charing Cross Road along Shaftesbury Avenue – on the right-hand side.

Jonny

There's *Incognico* in Shaftesbury Avenue (nearer Cambridge Circus, but not far) which has very good reviews (although I wasn't that impressed, but it might have been an off-day). I'm sure they do a pre-theatre menu. Further down the price scale is the *Italian Kitchen* in New Oxford Street and *Grape Street Wine Bar* (which does food), both of which are nice. Have a lovely time.

cfalconer

A great place for taking parents is *Joe Allen's* on Exeter Street, quite old fashioned (in a good way), great food, reasonable prices and there are always B-list celebs – there's always some old soak from *Coronation Street* in there. They often have a live pianist as well.

KK

Is Maiden Lane close enough? *Rules*, in Covent Garden: www.rules.co.uk.

Evil Dave

Lunch
Whilst recommending places for hearty lunches – try* BLT *on Great Eastern Street/Curtain Road. Daily specials, massive portions and a hangover-beating egg and bacon sarnie! Don't all rush at once though, the queues are bad as it is!

Woodenhorse

Another amazing place for lunch is Kastner and Ovens *on Floral Street in Covent Garden – next to the opera house. My colleagues and I are convinced they put a 'special' something in their food because everything tastes amazing and it's impossible to not go there every day!! They have daily specials and great salads and truly delicious pasties and quiches, along with an incredible selection of home-made cakes and pies...*

greedypig

ROOFTOPS

Now that the spring is in full swing, I'd like to know where London's best rooftop restaurants are at, please. I don't know where there are any and I need to get up there and eat, close to God. I'm starving.

Bo Jaxx

If you want to splash out and go Conran, *Coq D'Argent* at 1 Poultry near Bank is a rooftop restaurant and bar with panoramic views around the City. Be warned though, you may have to mingle with the dreaded Suits... no policemen though, Bo Jaxx.

Archie

Not rooftops as such, but a place where you can get a pretty good view. *OXO Tower* (the bar was good but the restaurant was overpriced, the space non-existent and the food uninteresting) and *Smiths of Smithfield* (top floor... duh) which has an outside terrace overlooking St Paul's etc. Beware though, *Smiths* is pricey and £28 for a steak is expensive even if you do get the donor's life story along with 8 mm cine film.

Juvey

Smiths of Smithfield (Charterhouse Street, just off
Farringdon Street) has an almost rooftop situation. Their
top floor has a glass wall and outdoor terrace with a Mary
Poppinsesque view over rooftops – lots of copper
domes, *St Paul's* and the *Old Bailey*. It's not cheap, but
nice for a treat. www.smithsofsmithfield.co.uk.

Bermondsey Gal

Aside from *Babylon* in Kensington, I'm not so sure about
rooftop dining in London – unless you know someone
who belongs to *Soho House*, which has an excellent roof
terrace. *Chez Gerard* in Covent Garden has a nice terrace
and there are at least four decent restaurants with al
fresco tables, *Thameside* on *Butler's Wharf* near Tower
Bridge, plus a few at *Gabriel's Wharf* near Waterloo
Bridge. And of course, there's always the *OXO Tower*
balcony (for a price) – but I recommend you stay inside
if it's a windy night. Enjoy!

lady at lunch (dreaming of it, anyway)

LATE NIGHT COFFEE

**This'll sound strange to some, but sometimes, what
I'd really like is to go out for a mellow coffee, and
maybe even an ice cream late in the evening (10ish
to midnightish)! I know there must be the perfect**

place for me in central or south west London –
somewhere you don't have to shout to be heard and
people don't look at you like you have three heads
when ordering caffeinated drinks at strange times of
day. Will any of you fellow coffee-lovers out there
help me?

coffee quest

I know exactly what you mean! My hubby and I have
been talking about this for years and if we could be arsed
would actually try and open a late night coffee and
dessert place. Unfortunately, we haven't and I don't
know of anywhere in south London, but it's just so nice
to know that other people think the same. If anyone
knows of anywhere in the Crouch End to Highbury area
we'd be most grateful. Good luck, coffee quest.

Margorah

Bayswater – there's loads of late night places open for
coffee and ice cream. Come out of Bayswater station,
cross over, turn left and about half way down (before the
Prince Albert pub) there's a good coffee shop that does
Häagen Dazs. Why you'd want ice cream in this weather
however...

Marmalade

In Soho around Old Compton Street there is a collection of late night coffee shops including *Bar Italia*, which is down Frith Street. Crowds of people usually fill the street on busy nights and especially between 12 and 3 a.m. Fantastic place.

laurie

I'd recommend the lovely *Café Ciao*, which is at 17 Charing Cross Road. Not only is it a nice, quietish place for a coffee, but they do utterly fabulous ice cream, including a few dishes that are designed to look like pasta dishes (e.g. 'spaghetti' made from vanilla ice cream with 'Bolognese' sauce made from strawberries). Well worth a trip, and open until late!

Flick

Try the little Italian gellati place just south of Leicester Square on the Charing Cross Road – REAL Italian ice cream and proper coffee. It's not loud, though the music does suck occasionally. Not sure if it or its coffee is mellow enough for you, but worth a try.

snapper

I used to put on club nights which involved a lot of late night rendezvous. A great place to hang out is a small cafe round the back of *fabric*, it's open all night for the clubbers

and the market sellers round there. Plus you
get to see everyone at each end of the spectrum, hard
grafters going to work and hard clubbers on their last legs.

12th Monkey

There's a nice café – *Sacred* – that recently opened in
Carnaby Street that serves drinks till 11 p.m. – delicious
organic coffee and specialty teas and it sometimes has
live (but mellow) music in the evenings. They aren't a
horrible chain and the inside is done up like a church.

toomuchcaffeine

Best place for late night coffee that I know is *Bar Italia* on
Frith Street – it is the closest thing to Italy that I know and
serves great coffee and delicious cakes and pastries. Just
don't go telling EVERYONE! To my mind it beats all the
overpriced bars hands down, plus you can actually speak to
your mate, rather than mouthing to each other...

Pinkle P

Rich

I've just inherited an enormous sum of money. I do intend to give a lot of it away, never fear. However, I also intend to piss a lot of it up the wall on superfine living and unnecessary extravagance. One of the things I've always wanted to do is spend more on a single meal than most people earn in a month, so I was wondering, what are some of the most expensive restaurants in London and what's the most expensive meal? Quickly now, at the rate I'm spending, I'll be skint by Sunday

Croesus

Not necessarily a meal, but Selfridges' food hall does an £80 sandwich. Wagyu beef, shaved white truffles and similar. And I'm sure their wine department just down stairs could knock a few notes out of your purse for a vintage bottle to go with it.

Goodjudge

TRANSPORT

LONDON IS... RETIRED ROUTEMASTERS and dodgy cab drivers; London is congestion, compensation and suicide; London is people blinded by selfishness; London is moments of life-affirming joy hitting you in the face when you least expect it and most desire it; London is shocking, lackadaisical and rude; London is the exception that proves the rule...

Most memorable tube experience?
'A pregnant lady asked a middle-aged man to open the little window because she felt faint. He refused to do it saying "the wind would blow through his hair". I have never forgotten that. What a twat.'

Emma Kennedy, actress and writer

THE UNDERGROUND

KANGAROO

Can any tube drivers/electrical engineers out there tell me why underground trains often do a 'kangaroo start' when they're moving off – a lurch that is often accompanied by a loud popping sound. District and Circle line trains seem especially susceptible to this – and usually when they're so crowded that standing passengers fall all over the place when it happens.

Llamapiss

I was once told that was the sound of the mice popping as they were run over – obviously it's not but that sound always makes me wonder...

I hate Wednesdays

Well, Llamapiss, I'm afraid the sudden lurching is not the driver trying to get a cheap laugh, but instead something much more dull... You see it is actually all us poor commuters' faults. When people are leaning against the doors of the carriage and the train starts to move off, sometimes their weight causes the door to open slightly. This in turn sets off the emergency brake system which cuts forward power at the same time. The popping noise is, I'm guessing, the hydraulic (or whatever) pressure being released by a valve (or somesuch). How do I know this incredibly boring bit of trivia? Erm... I just do. Nothing at all to do with the fact that it was my body pressing against the doors one day and subsequently made the tube jolt four or five times. To which the driver then commented, 'Will the prat who is leaning against the doors when we start to move please stop leaning against the doors when we start to move. I'm sure we would all appreciate getting to the next stop'. On second thoughts. It's the drivers just getting a cheap laugh.

Machine

Bad days

For a long time I've been astounded by the rudeness and selfishness of people on the tube. What has happened to a bit of courtesy and manners? I was on a packed Northern line train the other day (defective train somewhere or other) totally squished, when the train duly pulled in to Angel tube station. There was a guy next to me who was holding on to the ceiling rail, quite inconsiderately his arm was right in the space you might expect my head to occupy so I was already at an uncomfortable angle. He was more than aware of my presence; there was no way he could have not seen me. I considered asking him to move his arm slightly but more fool me I decided no, after all everyone was in the same boat, and was just glad I could now get off. So, ready to get off... and BAM! Mr Nob-Head decides he is also getting off at Angel and brings his arm and elbow down right into my face, sending my glasses flying at the same time. Now perhaps I am being too hard on him, maybe he was just a stupid dumb moron from whom we can expect no better, but the guy didn't even turn round to check that I was OK – off he rushes and it's only thanks to other people in the carriage having an ounce of decency and letting me scramble around on the floor to pick up my (pretty expensive I might add) glasses before someone equally pea-brained might stand on them, that I managed to recover them intact. And a big thank you to the one guy who did actually ask if I was OK. I'd hoped to have found the idiot who whacked me soon as I got off the tube but of course he'd been in such a hurry he was nowhere to be found. I hope he's reading this and feels incredibly guilty. As for me, I feel much better now. Thanks LbL for letting me vent!

Peedoffatselfishmoronsonthetube

I also feel very much for you Peedoffatselfishmorons-onthetube. One day whilst taking a leisurely trip on a rather packed tube, and being very close to the doors, we stopped at a station with a crowded platform. No one in the carriage was able to move an inch so obviously there was no room for anyone to get on but despite this a rather large man on the platform took the liberty of lifting me up and out of the tube (I am fairly small) to take my place. The doors promptly shut and he was whisked away on MY tube and I was left on HIS platform. Quite frankly I was shocked. This aside from all the barging and not waiting for people to get off and smelly armpits makes me very sad. THANK YOU to the few nice people I have met who have kindly waited and smiled and helped with luggage.

theyellowmule

Congestion

Interesting fact. TfL is actually creating congestion to encourage belief that the congestion zone is good. Traffic lights are staying on red longer and green shorter to build up traffic. If you ring TfL and complain they always say 'It's a fault' and it goes back to how it was for a few weeks before they tweak it again. When the International Olympic Committee was in town Ken had the light sequences changed so that traffic flowed and impressed the IOC. And did you know tourist coaches, not just buses and taxis, are exempt from congestion charging. Why should tourists be exempt when us locals have to pay?

CityGent

COMPENSATION

Having just spent yet another journey on a delayed tube train crammed full of angry, frustrated, halitosis-ridden, farting, idiot fellow commuters I

wondered whether anyone else bothers to fill in one of those compensation forms that are available at every station? It's just that as I finally reached my destination and grabbed one of the aforementioned claim forms I didn't see a single person amongst the hundreds of people streaming out of Canary Wharf station doing the same thing.

Does no one else know that if you're delayed for more than 15 minutes on any tube journey you can claim for compensation that amounts to half the value of the cost of your journey? Shit, you can even go online and do it at: https://www.tfl.gov.uk/tube/contacts/refunds.asp.

Don't give me that 'I haven't got time to fill out stuff like that' bollocks. It takes less than five minutes and believe me, it is so rewarding when you get the vouchers through your front door. Don't just bend over and let TfL do you up the chutney. Make them pay for making you late!

 *makethebastadspay*

makethebastadspay is quite right – you should do this every time you are delayed by 15 minutes or more. Last year I got more than £70 in TfL vouchers which I used against the renewal of my annual Gold Card. Small recompense for putting up with the Northern line every day!

BABY ON BOARD

I just wanted to get people's opinion on pregnant ladies asking people for seats. I am six months pregnant and up until now have found standing on the daily commute no problem at all. However, I am now starting to find it a bit of a struggle, especially when the tubes are busy and hot. My sister bought me a 'baby on board' badge which I don't  **feel comfortable wearing so have left it at home. However, not one person has ever offered me a seat, though lots of people have sat and stared at me. I therefore wanted to find out people's thoughts on asking for a seat and if you think I would be taking the piss by asking.**

 *Green Eyes*

Being charitable, I'd like to say that at six months people may be unsure as to whether or not you might just have eaten too many pies and be too embarrassed to assume. Or they may just be in cloud cuckoo land. That happens to me at times. But being realistic, I suspect they're just too selfish. When I see someone who needs a seat, and I'm standing, I ask someone seated 'can you let this person have your seat please?' and they usually jump up, embarrassed and apologising. I think if you ask politely, touching your tummy to make it clear the reason why you're asking, I suspect people will almost always give up their seats. I had the good fortune to be pregnant in a civilised (in some ways) city – Buenos Aires – and each time I got on the underground there several people would jump up at once and all would insist the others sat down. It was quite amusing. And in the post office queues etc., I would get ushered to the front. Good place to be expecting. Bad place to wheel a pushchair (but that's another story).

roobydooby

A friend of mine is about as pregnant as you are and she finds that if she pretends to read a pregnancy magazine (even a shockingly old one), people will notice and offer up their seats. Simple, yet effective.

The Figurative Pineapple

I've been offered a seat before by a very sweet little boy – and I'm just a bit fat.

Melee

For God's sake, wear your 'Baby on board' badge. How the hell are we supposed to know you're not just fond of your fry-ups? If you have a badge, wear it with pride. Or else, don't complain about people not being gentlemanly. They're staring at you because they're trying to work out whether you're pregnant or not, and whether you would be offended if you were not pregnant. You should feel sorry for these people (like myself) who are clearly in a quandary. Yes, ask them to get up if you need to, but please make it easier both on yourself and on your fellow commuters by wearing the badge! Apart from the obvious – more likely to get a seat on the tube – you won't have loads of people staring at you wondering whether you're obese or not. Sorry if I sound a bit rude (I don't mean to be, and I hope you have an amazingly wonderful and trouble-free pregnancy and a gorgeous healthy bouncing baby) but I just thought that if you don't wear the badge, surely you shouldn't expect people to assume you're pregnant. Wear the badge! Hugs.

Mestalla

Only thing with the badge though – wear it at hip height! I used to wear mine on my bag. That way it is at eye level to those people determined not to catch your eye. Gives them no excuse then! Good luck with the rest of your pregnancy and hope you have the courage to get a seat when you need it.

Pelepeg

Definitely wear the badge. I'm fat and it always works for me.

Just big boned

I'd recommend making an announcement as you get on – beggar style: 'I hate to trouble you lovely people this morning but I've had a bit of bad luck and got myself pregnant. All I need is a seat for twenty-three-and-a-half-minutes. I'd be ever so grateful. Thanks.' It might help if you smelled a bit too.

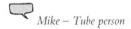
Mike – Tube person

WRONG

Is it just me, or are the escalators to the Northern line at Moorgate tube station completely the wrong way round? I instinctively head towards the left escalator (always standing on the right of course) only to be greeted with those mechanical wonders

**chugging up on the down side and down on the up.
Is there a reason for it? Do they ever go the other
way? Have you too boarded the wrong one whilst
rat-arsed and been flung unceremoniously across the
station on your arse? Thank the lord that beer makes
your bones bounce off concrete.**

enfant

I'm right with you. When that happened to me most
recently, I was slightly fuzzled, and couldn't quite figure
out how it came to be that there were people facing me,
coming down my escalator when it was going up. My
sincere apologies to the snogging couple, who found me
refusing to believe reality, and blocking their way as they
tried to disembark the escalator. Look, it's just really
confusing, alright?

Juvey

The escalators at Camden Town are arse about face
too... left one goes down, right side up. Even though I
use them every day I never noticed it until I read that
post.

Markus M

The escalators at Notting Hill Gate (to the Central line) seem to be the wrong way round too. But only if you're there to catch the first couple of trains. Many-a-time have I been caught out by the wrong-way-round escalators when blindly drunk at 6 in the morning. I think it's a joke by the CCTV operators and they just sit there and watch drunks falling over.

niddle

I use Bermondsey station and I swear every morning they are going in different directions. I think LU bods are just on a wind up. But then how bored must they be sitting in a tube station all day. Can't blame them really! We should be grateful they don't change the direction whilst in use. Oh, while we are on the subject of escalators, why does it still feel like they move when you step onto a stationary escalator – or is that just me?

Luc

MUSICAL LONDON

Every morning for the last week, we've been treated to some classical music on our way through Brixton station. Any reason for this? And does this happen at any other tube stations?

Darcy Sarto

Apparently I'm told that classical music is being played in various stations to calm people down so they show less aggression on their journey into work. It is also being played at Vauxhall station but it doesn't stop me wanting to punch people when they annoy me.

Classy girl

Apparently they first trialled the classical music thing in Vauxhall (I think) and found that it reduced the amount of vandalism and petty crime in and around the station, so they're extending the trial to other stations. A rather lovely idea, I think, as it's not intrusive and provides a nice soundtrack for the

journey if you're not lucky enough to have an
iWotsit.

babybat

Am I the only one who thinks the classical music in
Brixton tube lends it a certain unsettling Clockwork
Orangey Beethoven/threat of extreme violence combo?
Just me? That's OK then.

lostgeordie

No, you are not alone in finding the music wafting
through Brixton station a little unsettling. It reminds me
of *One Flew Over the Cuckoo's Nest* – I keep expecting
someone in the big glass office next to the ticket barriers
to go up to the microphone and say 'medication time'.
I'm sure it is a good idea though and it's just you and me
that are unnerved by it. Do come over to help me if
you find me in the corner of the station quietly
rocking.

Louby Lou

ONE UNDER

Depressed? Suicidal? Fine. Kill yourself. See if I care. But for God's sake, don't throw yourself under a tube train. Or if you do, by God, I will come and find your final resting place, I will dig you up, fistfuck your remains and burn them, you loathsome self-centred worm, you. Really though, there is no excuse for it and to end your life with such an incredibly selfish act – an act that will disrupt the lives of thousands, if not tens of thousands, of people – can only spell eternal suffering in the afterlife. Or worse still, an appalling fistfucking from me. I understand that it's almost certainly one of the quickest methods, and least likely to fuck up, but really – try and think of others for at least once in your life. And if you want a surefire alternative, come round to mine at a time convenient to both of us and I'll happily facilitate your demise with my bare, clenched hands. No charge.

Bo Jaxx

Totally agree with you, but I was under the impression that getting run over by a tube was not the quickest way to go. Apparently the wheels crush you and don't slice you into pieces. Most people are still alive and conscious when the firemen turn up and it's only when the tube is raised up that they then die of massive and sudden blood loss…!

p

A friend of mine died a few years ago having been sucked under a tube. I'm really pleased that 'p' has now given me all the gruesome details I wanted, and that everyone else in London hated him for being so inconsiderate as to make them late getting home from work. Aren't we a tolerant bunch.

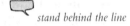

stand behind the line

For fuck's sake, 'stand behind the line', no one's having a pop at your unfortunate friend. And I'm sure that 'p' didn't think to him or herself before jotting down the details 'Gosh, I hope 'stand behind the line' reads this!' It's a conversation about how appalling it is to choose to take your life in a way that not only delays and frustrates thousands of commuters, but that also causes drivers, medics, clean-up crews etc., a lot of stress and sadness. Did anyone say they were including the accidental deaths in the fistfucking threat/debate? DID THEY? No. So just fuck off. You people wear me out with your incessant need to stick your grief in my face. Oh gosh. I've gone and been all intolerant. Whoops all over the place. Love and cuddles.

Pokeyozo

To 'stand behind the line' – your friend was sucked under a tube train? How? By what? Was there a giant worm under there – something like in 'Tremors'?

The Black Cherry

If you really think suicide has anything remotely to do with the everyday petty actions that are driven by selfishness, then you should probably be thankful for your ignorance. It's something superficially akin to selfishness, but it's in a whole other universe of feeling, or lack of it. I think it might be safe to say that anyone who throws themselves under a train isn't, er, really thinking straight. I mean, really. Selfishness is pretending not to notice a pregnant woman who really needs to sit down. I don't think it has much to do with a desperate act of violence against the self.

kote mass

One unders (or persons under a train as we like to tell passengers, to sound less gory) do happen often enough on the tube network. I am a tube driver on the Jubilee line and although I haven't actually had the misfortune of someone hurling themselves under my train, I have been on-scene to assist after such incidents and it's not a pretty sight. The recess under the middle rail is actually called 'a suicide pit' and it does offer some chance of surviving if you fall on the track. But you gotta be real lucky because apart from a train thundering into the platform around 40 mph, you have 630 volts running through the conductor rails, and that would pretty much make the getting run over by the train painless as you would have been zapped well before.

tubeguru

Suicide is painless, and it does bring on many changes. It does also make people late for work, which is tragic. If you are thinking about topping yourself, do ring the Samaritans. Have some compassion for yourself, because as some of the posts here demonstrate, you'll find precious little in London sometimes.

edna

MAGIC MOMENTS — THE JOY OF THE UNDERGROUND

Smile end

If you were at Mile End tube station on Saturday just before 8pm, you might have shared one of those lovely London moments, where something a bit odd happens, and people acknowledge their own and other travellers' shared confusion with a smile. Instead of the Central line tube I was expecting to pull up, a load of open carts carrying stones/coal passed the platform. I have certainly never seen the tube lines being used to transport bits of rock about. Is there some local mining going on, or have I just been hopelessly unobservant for the last seven years? Incidentally Earl's Court District line at about 7 pm on a Tuesday used to be another good time for catching other passengers' eyes and smirking. They test their sound system and you hear 'Sentence 7. What kind of shoes do the Indians wear?' and other such gems blast out of the loudspeakers. I have no idea why they use that tape, but it certainly brings District liners out in a smile.

coal spotter

I have it on good authority that that is, and I quote, 'Ballast heading for the open air sections between Epping and Stratford.' So there you go!

Tris2000

I was on the Jubilee line yesterday, trundling back to civilisation after another day pushing paper in Canary Wharf and had a driver giving us a running commentary on delays and the fallacy of signal failure. People peered up from their Dan Browns and the morning's *City AMs* and caught each other's eyes, momentarily bonded by the driver's assertion that the fact that we were stuck in the tunnel was because LU are simply 'rubbish'. The grey faces got a little coloured, and I think there was a brief sense of why we all bother in the first place...

alwayswatching

I'm curious to know – and it'd make a change from thinking about all the depressing/annoying/frustrating moments we've all had on the tube – what is the oddest/ most surreally entertaining sight you've come across on London's public transport? Possibly, mine is watching a guy trim his pet guinea pig's toenails on the Northern line on a weekday morning. (Needless to say it was after the rush hour, when obviously there isn't room to swing a cat, much less give a rodent a manicure.)

Carty

Best moment was looking up and noticing a very subtle sticker on the carriage wall – in perfect LU public info font, there was the message 'No Eye Contact – Penalty £200'. Brilliantly clever – took a photo and even sold it to *Nuts* magazine!

snapper

Blunt

At the risk of sounding like the Mayoress of Big Head Junction, I just wanted to say to the guy on the Piccadilly line this morning who mouthed 'you are beautiful' at me across the carriage before leaving at Leicester Square, that I apologise for responding by blushing furiously and firmly avoiding eye contact thereafter (I'm also sorry I made you repeat it three times but, hey, I'm not a lip reader). Anyway, to be perfectly frank, it was borderline creepy and let's face it, you can't be too careful. Having said that, my ridiculously fragile ego thanks you for the slightly guilty enjoyment I experienced from such flattery, no matter how much of an out and out lie it clearly was. So if you read this – thanks for the sweet, albeit slightly dubious, shot in the arm on such a rubbish Friday morning.

icarriedawatermelon

A few months back I was on a Smith and Shitty line train going westbound. A stop or two before Hammersmith (it may have been Goldhawk Road) a lady got a thin strap/piece of material from her rucksack caught in the doors as they shut. Now, because the material was so thin, the doors still shut and the train pulled away. But because her rucksack was on so tight, she was literally stuck to the doors and couldn't move. She said to anyone who'd listen that, 'It's alright, I'll move when the doors open at the next station'. But the doors opened on the other side at Hammersmith and I left the train chuckling as she hung around. Fnar.

Stevedore from Tyneside

A while back I was on a Northern line tube from Archway when it was delayed in Warren Street station – cue the driver saying, 'I apologise for the delay but this train is running a little early, and that is simply not tolerable on London Underground'. Sometimes these unsung heroes of LU humour make it all worthwhile.

nastychimp

I boarded a Circle line train from Baker Street to King's Cross to find a young lad sitting there with '80s style ghetto blaster mounted on his shoulder, listening to *Bryan Adams'* 'Everything I Do' (the *Robin Hood* movie one). Much to the mixed irritation/amusement of the carriage, he was soulfully singing along with gusto, and he also didn't appear to know where the bridging chorus 'There's no love like your love etc.' went, because he kept trying to insert it at various points in the song. At Great Portland Street a suited city gent got on, obviously wrapped up in what he was thinking about. As the train moved off he noticed the noise, looked over to see what was causing it, and upon seeing this guy he sort of rolled his eyes and mouthed a swearword – as if this was all he needed after a busy day. As he did this I made eye contact with him and a couple of the other passengers, and for a fleeting instant there was a conspiratorial snicker going on – it was one of the most beautiful moments of community I've ever felt on the tube. And the side effect being that all of us who got off at King's Cross, on the walk across to the Northern line, found ourselves involuntarily humming that bloody song, and you could quite audibly hear repeated and scattered mutterings of 'Everything I dooooo... fuck!' all the way to the platform.

mrfrisky

In the summer, just after the bombings, a tube driver announced: 'Please remember to take your luggage, litter and bombs with you to avoid unnecessary delays'. It shocked a few people but I appreciated the sense of humour.

Syren

A while ago I was on my train home from London to Kent, with my iPod in and nose buried in a book as usual, when I noticed the guy next to me was sort of shaking occasionally. I thought, 'Great I've got someone who's a bit weird next to me', but I soon realised he was chuckling and that this subdued mirth was being shared by several people in the carriage. I took out my iPod and discovered there was a rather strange man standing in the entrance way to the carriage making really loud, repeated fart noises with his mouth. He kept on doing it while people looked at each other and tried not to laugh – the girl in front of me was shaking and had tears down her face (there is, after all, nothing funnier than something you're trying not to laugh at). He stayed for about one stop and then moved onto into the next carriage, and when he left everyone in our section of the carriage laughed together and had little chats. It was lovely. He was either mad or doing his bit to entertain the commuting hoards and spread a little joy, or both. I preferred the latter and like to think I was proved right when a couple of months later a friend told me she had had the pleasure of his company on a journey too. More of these stories please!

Trampy Jane

One of my favourite London moments happened a few years ago when my then boyfriend was blowing some of his student loan on taking me out for a swanky meal for my twenty-first. We got a black cab from my college in Marylebone to the restaurant in Primrose Hill, and the driver chatted to us about where we were going (Odette's – great restaurant, by the way!) and what the special occasion was. We were amazed when he dropped us off outside the restaurant and told us we didn't owe him anything, and that we should put the cab fare towards the meal instead. What a lovely bloke! I've cherished that story ever since.

clarebear

Me and my mate were on a fairly busy tube recently, in the middle of the afternoon, somewhere on the Central line. This girl opposite – she was early 20s and looked perfectly normal to me – suddenly told my mate she thought he looked like Donny Osmond. We both laughed, and my mate said, 'do I 'eck' (we're northerners). The girl leapt from her seat, stamped her foot hard on the floor, and shouted, really, really loudly, and very angrily: 'YOU DO LOOK LIKE DONNY OSMOND! YOU DO! YOU DO!' And then she sat back down, looking all exasperated and tired of stupid people who don't agree that they look like seventies pop stars. We then sat in silence, until we got off a couple of stations later.

Ticoallstar

A man got on the Jubilee line train (I think at Kilburn) and proceeded to announce that talk of weddings made his guts bad. He then hunched down and proceeded to vacate his bowels to some loud and soggy sounds. No one said a word or even looked around as it was just too disgusting. Luckily for us all he got off a couple of stops later and had prepared for the episode by tucking his trousers into his army style boots so we weren't left with a reminder. Memorable!

sibslock

I was on the Northern line once and there was a not unattractive girl sitting opposite me reading the *Daily Mail*. A couple of stops later she was sick all over the paper. I like to think that was her comment on the contents of the newspaper rather than being drink induced. Also I saw Charles Kennedy on a tube to Kennington the other night. He had a very red face.

The Assassin Prince

I can outdo that... Busy carriage, late at night, around Christmas time so people are in penguin suits and ballgowns. A particularly beautiful nymph is sitting and drooping on a chair, fallen asleep. Her hands are on her lap and her head nods occasionally over her knees, flipping up occasionally. At a station that will remain anonymous, a drunk gets on. Not only is he drunk but he's homeless. And not only is he homeless, but he's in a very bad state. He almost has his own farm of flies. You can smell piss on him from a mile away. Anyway, he staggers along the carriage and stops by this beauty. He tries to focus, but he can't. But he can tell she's beautiful as she's sitting there in a blissful dream. Then his nose runs and a drop of snot lands on one of her hands – it's such a shock that it wakes her up. And it's even more of a shock that she doesn't want someone to think her nose was dripping so she surreptitiously licks it up. I can do worse, you know... But I thought this would help you if you're on a diet...

Potty Time

Sometime around 11 p.m., some time in the latter quarter of last year, a friend and I boarded a Northern line train at London Bridge, travelling southbound to Clapham South to go home, having already imbibed a fair skinful at the many quality hostelries in Borough. It was quite busy and so we were forced to stand in the double door vestibule that was mostly taken up by a bunch (about five or six maybe) of merry revellers, one of whom was clearly leaving her job with the others being her soon-to-be-ex-colleagues. Being slightly inebriated, they were chatting and laughing loudly among themselves and so, also being slightly inebriated, my friend and I got chatting with them. They were a nice and friendly crowd, and thus was formed a 'nice tube moment'.

Now, this sort of thing is pretty cool in itself, strangers talking and laughing together on the tube, but not all that unusual, especially at that time of night. However, the really cool part of the story comes a couple of stops later (Elephant or Kennington, I can't remember), when a girl in her early twenties gets on the carriage and into our jolly vestibule with a big hold-all bag. We welcome her into our the-tube-isn't-always-so-bad gang and she's soon chatting and laughing away with the rest of us. Suddenly she delves into her bag and produces a bottle of tequila and, having silently allayed any fears of potentially dissolved roofies by taking a swig herself first, invites us all to have a shot. Pretty cool, huh? Not everyone accepted, but I sure did and am living to tell the tale. All too soon Clapham South came along and my friend and I alight, for once actually sorry to be leaving a tube carriage.

uberrich

S-S-S-Scam

Last night I was approached last night by a stuttering chap dressed in the usual street person style save for a stethoscope around his neck. He claimed to be a doctor, whose colleague's car had broken down, and who needed to get to Acton. He needed 'just £5 for tube fare' to do this. Recalling the cautionary words of LbL readers I apologised for having no cash on me and strolled off. Seconds later a police car zoomed up with sirens going and the good doctor was bundled into the back. Judging by this pretty crap ruse, I think he's getting desperate.

Dan

ON THE BUSES

DISABILITY

Is it illegal for bus drivers to question passengers' disability (or apparent lack thereof) when fit young men get on and use their orange Freedom Pass on London buses? I am gobsmacked how I have never seen any of the young men challenged ONCE over their card, which is blatantly in its orange 'Freedom Pass' wallet, and which shows 'F'DOM PASS' on the display when swiped on the bus. I've been watching. Just yesterday, a fit athletic-looking young man jumped onto the bus, did not appear to have any learning difficulties and certainly no physical difficulties... What I want to know is, how come these things don't appear to be challenged. I'm not saying that these Freedom Passes are necessarily all fraudulent misappropriation of granny's card – and some of these young men may indeed have a disability of their own that is not immediately apparent – but surely drivers are allowed to check or ask, without fearing to cause offence in any way? Are bus drivers forbidden from asking why an apparently mentally and physically fit young man is using a Freedom Pass?

Tris2000

Lots of my patients get them issued to them by their community support workers (I'm a psychiatrist) – so these apparently fit young men may have got them via that route. Contrary to what the *Daily Mail* and *Evening Standard* etc., report, most people with mental illness aren't the slobbering, dangerous, screaming, mass-murdering individuals they'd like you to believe. So I guess it wouldn't be fair to challenge people with them. Obviously it may not be the case with these guys, and they may just be being naughty. Just thought I'd give me two-pence worth.

Mister Ginger

Have you any idea how hard it is to qualify for one of those passes? I've just had to fill in a bloody long form (ten pages or so) answering all sorts of impertinent questions, and trying to get my social worker to pull his finger out and write a supporting letter. They are not just for the obvious, physical disabilities, but also for those of us suffering long-term mental illness. We don't all dribble, most of us look quite 'normal'. The young man in question may have been entitled to his pass for any number of good reasons that you can't see. Don't be so quick to judge.

daft vader

Tfl text

Transport for London run a text service that is supposed to tell you bus times. You text the service, you get your times (or that's the idea). Simple. Here are a few of the text messages that TFL's text service received recently, simultaneously revealing the extent of despair at London's bus service and also, a need for love and affection by many a cold, lonely Londoner:

- *Chas Where r u babe danny*
- *Again i requested these times earlier to day. They ard no good to me now*
- *CAN I PLS HAVE THE LATEST TRAVEL INFO*
- *WHY ARE THE 79 BUSES NEVER ON TIME. AND YOU GET TWO OR THREE 186s TWO OR THREE 340s BEFORE AND 79 COMES ALONG. I AWAIT YOUR ANSWER. TANKS GORDON*
- *Um stranded in one of your halts when a 288 didn't stop when I waved at the driver. Maybe he was practicing racing in the streets when he sped away. I would really appreciate if you could look into this matter*
- *Salut marie pierre;-) je t'appelle tout Ã... l'heure\J'espÃ... re que tu vas bien\Bisous\ Gaby*
- *Dude i am on a 48 number bus that right?*
- *Every seven minutes my arse*

- *Goats*
- *How about i aint intrested in bus times... i only want you my love... i want to lick your timetable and fondle your shelter...*
- *Is there a way to be Doctor Octopus on Spiderman 2 for the PS2*
- *You didn't text me you bitch of a bus stop... have you got a lampost i dont know about??! Its OVER between us!!!! Love you... bye!*
- *Is this the happy palace Chinese. I'd like to order a Chinese please, 114 chicken chow mein, 79 curried sauce, don't forget ma crackers this time! For 9p.*

edna

WEDDING BUS

I saw a fantastic open-top classic London Bus outside the registry office on Upper Street on Saturday. I'd like to get the same sort of thing for my wedding but I didn't go storming onto the bus to ask for the company name as I didn't think this was appropriate as the newlyweds were just about to

hop on. Do any LbLers know of any good companies for this sort of thing?

xforxray

Some friends got an open-top from this place – driver was great, terribly lenient about smoking/drinking/waving absurd inflatable dolphins at shoppers etc.

www.timebus.co.uk.

Have a top day anyway...

ils

Three suggestions for you:

www.ensignbus.com – speak to Nick Pirie

www.bigbus.co.uk

www.theoriginaltour.com.

Depending on time of year, you may find that only Ensign will have a bus available as the other two will make more money doing the round London tours. Ensign are currently charging me £750 for a period bus for six hours or so for a corporate evening job if that gives you an idea of costs. Best of luck.

Bo Tocks

I have just booked myself a Routemaster for my wedding in August – the company I used are called International Coaches and are based in Thornton Heath. For £380 + £35 for decorations (balloons, ribbons etc.) the bus will be picking me, hubbie and guests up and taking us from the church in Upper Norwood to our reception venue in Canary Wharf. Very good deal compared with other places I tried that attempted to charge £600+. Check their website out: www.internationalcoaches.co.uk, or call 020 8684 1011 and speak to Louise – she was very helpful and got the paperwork out to me really quickly.

Jojo

Zombie

Shocking? Lackadaisical? (Good word.) How about most London bus drivers? Top of my list would have to be the woman of substantial girth who sits morosely behind the counter at Maida Vale tube station. In all the times I've encountered her not once has she said hello, or thank you, or even acknowledged my existence. She just sits there like some outsized, jewellery-clad zombie. I'm torn between frustration, offence, and a genuine (if slightly

pompous and patronising) sympathy for someone
whose life appears to be so utterly joyless.

lessthanbeingfree

ROUTEMASTER REDUX?

**Was the whole Routemaster going out of service
lark all a rubbish hoax? I only ask because I nearly
choked on my Curly Wurly when I saw a passenger-
carrying Routemaster yesterday by Ludgate Circus.
Forget the route number but I stared at the female
ticket conductor inquisitively as it waited at the
traffic lights and she gave me a wry grin in return.
Do they dig them out if there's a shortage of
'normal' buses? Eh?**

Stevedore from Tyneside

The Routemaster is now used on London Heritage
routes only, mostly for tourists. The routes are parts of
the normal 9 and 15 bus routes, but contained within
central London. They've also been painted the way

buses were in the '60s, with original logos and everything!

temping for TfL has its bonuses...

THE ROUTEMASTER — RIP

Did anyone else go play play on the buses on the last days of the Routemaster? I did, and was very glad I did so. As I sat on the last-but-fourth 159 up from Streatham

through Brixton and Lambeth, it was cold and foggy and I thought 'hmm... I'm on a bus'. But then we crossed Westminster Bridge, the sun came out and they were waving and cheering and clapping us all the way up to Marble Arch. So, instead of going to do some Christmas shopping, I decided to join the queue for the return journey. I got on the last-but-two bus back, and it was marvellous. More love from the tourists, locals and enthusiasts all the way back to Streatham, and I don't think there was a throat without a lump in it as we raced another 159 up Brixton Hill while being cheered by schoolkids who'd been let out for the occasion so they could

wave flags and arms at us. Gawd bless the big stinky red bus.

iSleepDiagonal

That sounded brilliant. I took my 2-year-old to ride the buses on the last day of the No. 19 in Highbury, so at least I could tell her she'd been on them when she grows up. Then went home and had a sniffle to myself. Damn and blast Scroogey Ken and his Transport for London cronies. When's the next mayoral election due...?

Highbury Gal

Well that's a fine story, and I don't begrudge you your love for the RM. I myself had a soft spot for the 38 tempered, however, by the following observations:

1. The 'end of the Routemaster' has been strung out for like a year by various media outlets, to the point where I really could not take any more blathering about the bloody thing.
2. All the Routemasters are really quite old and dirty and knackered and handicapped inaccessible, and needed to be replaced (though obviously not by the Bendy Bitches).
3. It's only a bus.

RIP indeed.

Master Route

The good bus driver

A couple of months ago I was in Neasdon, a totally unfamiliar part of London for me. Somehow, trying to navigate using an A–Z and local buses, I got incredibly lost. I had a meeting in Southwark to get to, and as the time moved steadily towards it, I got more and more frustrated. Finally, walking along a lonely and deserted road underneath the North Circular, I just started sobbing like a five-year-old with a skinned knee. At this point, an empty bus appeared and stopped alongside me. I expected the driver to yell at me for walking in the road, but instead, he asked very kindly if I was OK. Like a child lost in a supermarket, I wailed 'I'm loooosssst!' The driver let me get on the bus without even asking to see my travel card, and, even though he was at the end of his route, let me wait while he did a loop round a supermarket car park to start again. While he did this he listened to me bemoaning my missed meeting and reassured me that I probably wouldn't be sacked if I explained what had happened (he was right too!). He then gave me several travel options to get back home and, when he finally left the bus in the middle of the journey, explained the whole situation to the new driver. Generally, I tend to find London bus drivers rather rude and unhelpful, but this one has a heart of gold. I can't even remember what route this all happened on now, but if a North London bus driver finds any of this familiar, thank you so much for rescuing me!

H of Brockers

Two wheels good, two wheels bad

NEW CYCLIST

Was given a bike, have just discovered cycling in London and am riding here, there and everywhere. Have bought panniers, a lightweight stack-hat, flashing lights and a bright yellow waistcoat (perfect for hitting those hardcore raves of an evening, too) as very much don't want to die. Would appreciate words of advice on what to do and not to do (am not going through red lights on point of principle – don't care how much of a wanker that makes me

sound) – stuff that other cyclists wish they'd known before the grotty white lorry knocked them over, that kind of thing. Not interested in pissing people off but want to know what's acceptable, and what's just going to spark car, pedestrian or bus rage.

SimoneMichelle

In reply to SimoneMichelle's (two names for the price of one!) post, here's 10 top tips:

1. To master London traffic, ride fast and alert. No music in the ears or lazily cruising along.
2. Don't cycle in the gutter, ride at least one metre out from the kerb – it forces other road users to actually do something to get past you rather than try to squeeze past.
3. Never undertake (pass on the left of) a large vehicle, like a bus (bendy or otherwise) or truck. Many of the cyclists that get seriously injured or die do so through getting caught between a large vehicle and a hard place. They can't see you – so overtake them on the right like everyone else.
4. In the damp or wet watch out for manhole covers – they are metal and incredibly slippery. Try to ride over them with your front wheel vertical – i.e. not turning.
5. Put skinny tyres on your bike. Through the winter I have been commuting with 21mm (less than an inch)

wide near-slick tyres – it makes it a more enjoyable, more satisfying experience. You don't need mountain bike tyres (the chunky, knobbly ones) on roads. 23–25mm semi-slicks should suit most riders.

6. Ride assertively. You have as much right to be on the road as anyone else, and by being assertive and consistent you force other road users – i.e. cars – to respect you and not take the piss.

7. Watch out for pedestrians. Sometimes it seems that London's pedestrians are a suicidal bunch, frequently walking out directly in front of you – this is because many people rely on their hearing when they're crossing the road, and they can't hear you coming. The only accidents I've had in 17 years of cycling on London's roads have been with pedestrians doing this.

8. Watch out for car doors opening onto you. Assume that a parked car has someone in it and they are about to open their door. Cycle outside this range.

9. When you know what you are doing and feel confident, put clipless pedals on your bike. They allow you to be much more efficient and it means your pedalling stroke is better for your knees (less up-and-down, more round-and-round).

10. Don't try to do what bike couriers do. They are the coolest cyclists around, but are complete nutters and pride themselves on taking incredibly high risks. (Most couriers now ride fixed-wheel track bikes, many of which don't have brakes.) When people say 'go play with the traffic', couriers take this as an

enjoyable challenge. For them it is a game, for the rest of us the risks just ain't worth it.

wheelie saying something

SCOOTERING

Anyone got any tips for me? I cycle to and from South Tottenham to Soho every day (6.5 miles each way) and quite frankly my thighs are getting a little muscly for a female (bigger than my boyfriend's now) and sometimes I just can't be arsed. I am tempted by a small 50cc scooter (Piaggio Zip I think) but am a tiny bit scared by the idea! I don't drive and took a CBT about two years ago which I passed but didn't feel confident as I had never been on the road before so I didn't get a bike. Now I have cycled for a year I'm wondering if I might not be a bit more confident with being on the road and hence it might be the way forward? My bf going on about how dangerous it will be freaks me a little too – I know it is on a bicycle too but he reckons the extra speed you get on a scooter makes a big difference with nasty accidents. I would just take a CBT and see but £95-odd is a little steep for an experiment! Someone tell me what to do! Give me some accident stats or something! Thanks.

milkandtwo

About 10 years ago a nurse told me once that the nickname hospitals use for people who ride motorbikes is 'organ donors'. But things may have changed.

natty head girl

Having moved from Bethnal Green to Crouch End I found myself faced with a tripling in transport costs to get to my work place in the Docklands (gone from a two-zone bus card to a three-zone travelcard) and decided to look into getting a scooter. Vespa are doing a great deal at the moment – 0% financing or 3.9% financing with a smaller deposit. This means that my monthly travel costs are cheaper than LU, and I have a lovely new scooter to be proud of. As long as you're sensible on the roads, then there is no reason to be scared. Go for it.

Griff

I felt the same a couple of years ago. My advice is to do a refresher CBT and then take yourself on a few trial journeys when it's safer. I practised around the city on Sundays when the bankers aren't there – it's dead apart from Spitalfields. I also did a few runs around my neighbourhood after work to get used to streets I knew in darker conditions. You will probably fall off or have a scrape but better to do so in your trial runs than on your way to work. I was fine once I'd got my confidence up.

Final tip – don't think you're still on the bicycle and put yourself at the very inner edge of the road – other drivers will fuck you up.

pippylongstocking

I don't think you need to know the statistics of road deaths on mopeds to London, but be proud to know that you are part of the very small proportion of people who keep themselves actively fit. Just think, what's more important, your legs being a little bigger and you living a healthy life, or travelling the short distance the lazy way and slowly turning yourself into a statistic of the ever-growing epidemic of people who do not exercise any more?

Will

I ride a 50 cc Piaggio Zip from Crouch End to Covent Garden every day and I love it. Upsides: not being dictated by bus/tube/train times; getting exactly where you want to go; spending £200 a year on petrol instead of the £1,000 zone 3 travel pass; feeling smug as you whiz past the queues at bus stops. Downsides: constantly having bad 'helmet hair'; carrying around helmet/jacket/fluorescent vest paraphernalia all the time. Worst of all is the other psychotic drivers on the road. I think that as you've been cycling you will have experienced these maniacs already. They cut across in front of you or pull out and just pretend you aren't there. The bonus with being on a scooter as opposed to a cycle is that you can go at the same speed as the traffic and not be pushed out into the gutter by greedy cars and trucks. I feel safer on the scooter than I ever did on a cycle. You just have to ride very defensively. You have to think that every vehicle hasn't seen you and is about to cut you up. That way when they do, and they invariably do, you are ready for it. As far as the speed goes, I rarely get over 35 mph because it's all traffic. One final note, please don't turn into one of those crazy scooter riders that give us a bad name by weaving in and out of traffic causing accidents in their wake.

Petal

I've had a Vespa for about two years and here are my pearls of wisdom:

1. You can never stop concentrating, even for a second. This is actually more difficult than it sounds. However, reminding myself how I am constantly close to death or having every bone smashed to smithereens usually helps keep my mind on the job.
2. It is significantly more dangerous than anything else I've ever done. What's most annoying is that, in a fight between a moron in a car and you on a scooter, the moron will *always* win. Not good for the ego.

3. When it rains, that danger gets quadrupled.
4. Don't get a 50 cc bike – the acceleration isn't enough to get off the lights quickly – you'll regret it. Try a 125 cc.
5. Buy a fur-lined granny blanket to protect you from rain and cold – they're an absolute essential.
6. Apart from the weather, the danger, and the trouble finding places to park in central London, having a scooter is completely brilliant. It costs £5 a week to fill up, £15 a YEAR in tax, and at around a grand for a second-hand Vespa, you'll make your money back within a year.

nnn mediummac

AND THE REST

SILVERLINK

Ah, Silverlink Metro. Unfortunately, being the way up it is, all the luck's fallen out of the horseshoe and the line is shit – plagued by cancellations, delays, murders and the most annoying tannoy system *ever*. After a particularly tiresome timewasting episode involving three train cancellations and a compound of 43 minutes of additional delays between Canonbury and Gospel Oak the other day, I had

plenty of time to rack my brains for the nickname this line has earned. It might be the 'Loony Line' but I'm sure there's one that is much more damning and satisfying. Do any fellow sufferers of this fickle form of transport know?

stella

I share your pain Stella, although not for much longer cos I've just moved to South Wimbledon so will be Northern-lining it from now on, but will miss the Silverlink Metro for all its aggro, carriage fights and delays of 400 minutes (surely that's just about 26 individual cancellations?). Nicknames though... I dunno, I just stick to the rather obvious Silvershite Hasbeen. Didn't know it had an 'official' nickname. Anyways, TfL are taking it over from Silverlink soon, not that that will improve anything...

Hairy Leper

We call the Silverlink the 'Rape and Murder Line'. Not particularly catchy or funny, but sums up the sort of vibe you get from it if you ever have to ride it at night.

silverlink escapee

It's called the Great North London Free Line as there was never anyone checking tickets or ticket barriers (might have changed now – been in South London for a while). Also, more romantically, my dad refers to it as the Chimney Pots Railway or something like that.

Ticket to ride

I've got a couple of beauties about that old slither-link! One of the best things I've ever heard it called is the Marrakesh Express by some bloke, which had the carriage chuckling. Second, I was waiting at Gunnersbury station for an eastbound slither the other day (as per usual it had been cancelled/delayed for at least 40 minutes) when a Silverlink pulled in going the other way to Richmond. A commuter waiting for an eastbound service innocently asked the driver (very politely) if the just-pulled-in-train would be terminating here and heading back eastbound (it happens sometimes). The driver's response? 'Shut up, you twat.' Then he drove off!

captain flamingo

Stella, your post brought back (well not fond really, just) memories of getting the (Pikey Line/North London Free Train) across town. It stops in some great places – and at each of those places seems to suck in all the resident loons and deposit them, white lightning, instruments, psychotic episodes 'n all, on the seat next to you. I'm sure there must be other nicknames for it but these are the two we used to use.

Rando The Mathemagician

It's not particularly snappy, but I've become accustomed to calling it 'The Slowest And Most Pointless Train In The Universe' (as opposed to 'The Most Expensive Train In The Universe' – the Heathrow Express). I used to have a recording on my mobile of an announcement by that disembodied bitch on the pole they have – 'The 6:31 to North Woolwich is delayed by approximately 77 minutes. Silverlink apologises for this late running, and any inconvenience it may cause you'. I swear, if I ever meet her in person I'm not going to be responsible for my (incredibly violent) actions. They might as well just put over a message that says, 'Ha ha ha, our train's shite, and we don't really give a flying fuck about you peasants! Keep waiting, and I hope it rains!' It really makes you appreciate the tube more though.

mrfrisky

THE GOOD CABBY

Left my snazzy (not available in UK yet) digital camera in a black cab on Friday night. A disbelievingly easy (didn't even put me on hold) phone call later, and it's found! Waiting for me at

the TfL lost property office! Thank you, cab driver! Just thought you should hear a good news story.

thenshesays

I worked in the Lost Property Office a few years ago for a very short period of time, no more than a fortnight, if I recall. I remember that in my very short spell of service, FIVE DIDGERIDOOS were handed in. The plus point to this is that if you are so addled that you leave your didgeridoo in a cab or on a tube, this means you probably won't get round to phoning up the Lost Property Office, hence saving us all earache from your crappy attempts at playing the thing. Hooray!

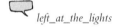

left_at_the_lights

CAB QUERY

I got in a cab the other night, and he didn't put the meter on (said he forgot), then tried to charge me about double what the normal price is. We had a stinking argument, but in the end, I paid up (just two quid less than he demanded). I had no choice, as I was a single female locked in a cab in the middle of the night. Question is, is there anything I could have done? I'm pretty annoyed, the whole reason you pay the extra for a black cab is their reputation.

Schotty

I had a not-outright-criminal but similarly annoying minicab experience the other day when booking a cab to take me to the airport. I rang up and asked for a quote based on my address, and booked on the basis of the quote I was given (£21). When I got to Heathrow and handed it over, the driver said I'd misunderstood because their prices *started* from £21, and demanded an extra £5, which I paid. Okay, so it was *only* an extra fiver, but I think I'd probably have been justified in refusing to pay considering I'd asked for a quote and spelt out my full address and postcode *before* they told me the price. (I was a wimp and paid up because I was a girl on my own in the middle of the night.) I don't know whether I was misquoted in the first place or simply overcharged, but LbLers, please approach Airport Express cabs on 0870 202 0555 with caution...

Cabsumer Champion

If anyone is ever in the situation you were in you need to tell the driver you will take their taxi licence number which is always prominently displayed in the back of the cab and will report them to the licensing authority (which is the Metropolitan Police in London). If you do this I suspect that you would suddenly find that they were a lot more reasonable about the whole situation. Sorry to hear you had a bad experience.

Eli

No cab driver 'forgets' to put the meter on by accident.
It's surely an automatic routine. It would be like you
having a shit and forgetting to wipe your arse. The fact
he overcharged you means that he quite clearly and
calculatedly tried to pull a fast one, especially with you
being a girl on your own at night. You should have
asked for a receipt and then jotted down the badge
number (on the window between you and him, and on
the back bumper), vehicle plate licence number and
registration number (these last two are also on the back
of the car). The likelihood is that if he saw you do this he
would suddenly become extremely compliant and
charge you the going fare, as cabbies do not like
investigations from head office. But assuming he doesn't
back down, make sure you complain to 020 7230 1631
and give them all this information. They will investigate,
they will remunerate you in some way if malpractice is
proven, and they will take action against the cabbie. Do
make it clear though that you do not want the cabbie to
have your home address, for obvious reasons.

 Tris2000

My dad's a black cab driver and I know that black cab
drivers are all scared of the police because getting into
trouble means losing their licence (and therefore their
livelihood). Let's hope there isn't a next time (I would
like to think he is a bad apple) but if there is, demand to
be driven to the nearest police station to get the police to

arbitrate. Alternatively his cab number should be displayed inside and on the rear of his cab (or get his badge number – probably hanging round his neck) and you can complain to the carriage office (www.tfl.gov.uk/pco).

wheels

Cab moment

I have a rather nice story for you. My work recently arranged for a dial-a-cab to pick me up from Waterloo after a business trip and so the cabbie had a placard in the window with my name on it. When I got into said cab the lovely driver asked if I was related to Henry Knatt (with 'Knatt' being my surname) and it turned out (to cut a long – and probably very boring for the rest of you – story short) that the cabbie used to work with my Grandad many years ago! Well, any of you who have family no longer around, it's lovely to hear stories like that, and it really cheered up my evening.

TK

HANG ONTO YOUR GOLD CARDS

I have just bought an Annual Gold Card/Season Ticket. I was advised at time of purchase that if it was lost/stolen, it would be replaced at a £10 admin charge. However, if it was lost/stolen again (which would be just my luck!), it cannot be replaced a second time! Surely this can't be true???

JingJing

It is true I'm afraid. Although I've never been unlucky enough to lose it twice, a few years ago when I had a Gold Card (it cost £6 if you lost it then), I lost my wallet and had to reapply and then go through an interrogation from a member of LUL staff to make sure I wasn't trying to skank them. The whole process took a couple of weeks, but I was allowed to claim back my travelcards in the meantime. They made me feel like a bit of a criminal though, and warned me then that if I lost it again I was basically buggered. Needless to say I guarded it with my life from then on. On another note I hope you're taking advantage of the one-third discount out of zone for you and up to four adults when you buy train tickets – took me bloody ages to find that out – and the discount is bloody good, like having a student rail card again.

Clefty

I recently got a Gold Card for the first time and I too was told I could lose it only once and would have to pay the full cost to replace it a second time. I got told all this when I was enquiring about the card. When I actually went to buy the card I asked the guy that sold it to me and he said that is strictly true but if you get a crime report then they should be able to help you out. Therefore, I don't think, for the sake of your bank balance, you should ever admit that you just lost it — always report it and get a crime reference number from the police and therefore it's listed as stolen and they will replace it! (This is what the man told me, I'm sure some other LbLer's will know if this is true or if they've had similar experiences.)

BB25

BB25 – reporting something you lost as stolen and getting a crime report is wasting police time (not to mention fraudulent if you are claiming a free travel card), and as a consequence illegal. Clowns that forget their phones in a pub, or can't be bothered to keep a travel card safe and then think they'll beat the system face prosecution to more than the value of what you have lost. Worth it? I think not. Also doesn't help that some poor sod of a copper has to fill out endless paperwork rather than getting on with something useful. You lose it, you pay for it. Take some responsibility for goodness sakes, and then when people really are victims of crime, they might get the support and help that they deserve, rather than being treated with suspicion and as a timewaster. Sorry for ranting at you but this really gets my goat.

Eveninall

Eveninall, you're wrong. You say that reporting something as stolen when you're not sure this is the case is 'wasting police time' and 'illegal', and quote 'clowns that forget their phones in a pub' as an example. Well if you forget your phone in a pub (or it drops out of your pocket), then ring the pub to see whether anyone has handed it in and if they haven't, then that constitutes theft. Are you suggesting that finders-keepers applies if you find something of value that is not yours?

Mestella

Fuckin' police. Chill out, pig. 'Wasting police time' – you trot that line out like you – more than anyone else – have a right not to have your time wasted. (Well, you do, legally, but I'm not so sure it's appropriate.) I suppose the idea is that when you're not having your time wasted, you're out there saving people's lives and arresting playground crack dealers. Yeah right. If only that were the case. Sadly, it's more a case of when you're not having your time wasted, you're out on the streets shooting innocent people in the face and laughing while black people choke in front of you. Balls to you.

Bo Jaxx

Bo Jaxx – run for Mayor would you. You'd get my vote. Respect.

plurks

Bo Jaxx – be honest. How long ago was it? And what did you get the fine for?

Keyworker

LOOPHOLE

Just before Christmas I remember reading an article in the *Standard Lite* about how a woman had successfully challenged one of TfL's penalty fares on a bendy bus, and exposed a loophole in the legality of fare evasion. Googling has found nothing useful, and unsurprisingly there's no reference to the case on TfL's website! I imagine that if I could find the woman's name I'd be able to see the court transcripts, but I can't remember! Can anyone help? I'm not planning to do anything illegal, since I have a yearly travel card, but I'd like to add some weight

to my argument that bendy buses are a waste of money...

Babybat

The case you are after is Francesca Knox v Transport for London, heard at Brent Magistrates Court. It should be possible to obtain more information on this case, including probably the defending solicitor's details, by contacting the Results and Orders Unit at Brent Magistrates Court. You will need to write a letter stating your reasons for wanting the information and pay a fee of £8.

What-a-Mess

I did a little search on one of those journalist websites that I have access to and I found Babybat's article. She was taken to court over an unpaid £1.20 fare on a bendy bus, when she mistakenly thought she had her ticket with her – she'd left it at home. After a ten-month wait, her lawyer successfully argued that penalty fares, according to the 1990 Public Services Vehicles Act, cannot be applied to the open-access buses which were introduced in 2001. In other words, bendy buses with more than one door are exempt. The end of the article does, sadly point out, 'TfL is expected to review its penalty fares policy'. Mind you, that happened on 19

December 2005. You might be able to fare dodge for a while – if you're that sad and hard-up!

robram

C-CHARGE

Am I the only person who thinks the congestion charge is a good thing? I think it should be raised from

£8 to £80 for the privilege of driving around town for a day, and anyone driving any kind of SUV/4x4 should go to the wall screaming, and I fucking mean that. The biggest plague in this great city is not pigeons, urban foxes, cute toddlers tripping us all up, intolerant unloved childless go-getters, or even visiting yanks. It's the TRAFFIC, without question. Consequently, anything designed to combat traffic can only be on the whole a positive thing (with the possible exception of the bendy bus). My question to you my fellow Londoners is this: what other workable measures can Ken, or anyone for that matter, introduce to make life worse for urban drivers?

Billy the Bull

Billy, sleep easy in the knowledge you're not the only person who thinks the congestion charge is a good thing. I do too and am happy to pay £8 now and again for the occasional use of my car in town. An increase to £80/ the death penalty, however, seems slightly excessive even by Red Ken's standards. I'd like to add that these horrid 4x4s are as much of an abomination outside the inner city as they are in London. Try driving down a village road (*not* a dirt track) with one of those Toad of Toad Halls coming at you as if they own the place. Totally unnecessary. I think a much better solution would be to get rid of them all. Perhaps round them up and have a public register of SUV offenders? Just a thought.

 calm down dear it's just an SUV

Yes, agreed. I think you are mistaken to single out 4x4 vehicles. This makes it too easy for people to start arguing that they are no bigger than a large family saloon car, as if that makes it all OK. Let's get it straight, any large vehicle is not only, in the most part, unnecessary, but also hugely impractical in the tight spaces of London streets. Yes they are getting more efficient, but they will never be as efficient as a small car and they will never have the same freedom of movement in tight streets. My parents brought up three boys with the aid of a tiny Fiat. Yep, it could fit a weekly shop in and push chairs and no it didn't need built-in Playstations to keep us happy. Please stop with the excuses! Anyway, all the arguing won't change the fact that we are running out of space; more and more people are buying cars, and petrol engines are killing the world. We are not scaremongering. This is really happening.

ECOWarrior

Walking through Forest Hill the other day, it was sunny, the air was filled with blossom, and I thought, this would actually be quite pleasant if it wasn't for all the goddam TRAFFIC. Zoom zoom zoom constantly without a break. Imagine if it was all horse and carts and bicycles and trains (lots of them! Clean, swift, electric numbers) and motorised transport was limited to emergency vehicles and maybe the odd bus. I'm not joking. I think our quality of life in London would improve immeasurably. With any luck, the coming oil crisis will mean that more people will have to abandon their cars anyhow. GOOD. The only thing wrong with the congestion charge is that it's too low and doesn't extend far enough.

Rosalba O'Brien

Billy the Bull is full of bull. The biggest problem people have with the 4x4 is that it has become an icon of wealth and God knows we all hate people who have done well financially and can afford something we can't. This blanket prejudice – albeit against a form of transport – is just another form of social intolerance and society scapegoat for things we struggle with like global warming.

For Chrissake please don't pander to the sandalled underclass with posts about 'statistically you are x times more likely to be injured if hit by a 4x4...' because the bigger the vehicle the more likely you are to be hurt if it hits you – we all tolerated everything from the mini to the Rolls Royce with engine sizes and emissions that would make a Range Rover's eyes water and no one complained until some journo coined the term Chelsea Tractor and hurrah! the have-nots have got something else to bleat about.

And as for the fucking C-charge – it's a grossly unfair tax on essential workers who can't afford to live in central London and are off the transport system anyway, and the biggest cause of business closure within its boundaries for decades.

Lan Drober

How irate you make me. I don't see the 4x4 as a symbol of wealth at all, in fact exactly the opposite, more a sign of stupidity. Having lived in London for ten years I've yet to discover exactly where the hills, fords, farmlands and general rugged terrain are that these vehicles are designed for. I couldn't agree more with Billy the Bull and his comments, you're a breed this suffocating planet could well do with out. As for the C-charge, hoik it up I say, Londoners deserve cleaner air, safer streets and far less social aggravation.

dickdasterdley

Lan Drober – your ridiculous twittering about 'prejudice and intolerance' is about as convincing as the Countryside Alliance's recent conversion to the 'Human Rights' cause, the BNP professing to love 'Freedom of Speech', or me bringing a porno home 'just to laugh at how stupid and fake it is'. This isn't about intolerance for the moderately wealthy – good for you! – it's about intolerance for the selfish and the ignorant. The only way you can possibly claim the moral right to drive a 4x4 and burn that much filthy petrol under everyone else's noses is if you're a farmer. Are you a farmer?

Mr Lizard

The truth is that *all* cars contribute to environmental issues. Picking on one type suggests that others are OK. These things really *are* happening, the planet *is* heating up, the roads *are* getting clogged with drivers and oil *will* run out one day. The answer is to ban all non-commercial traffic from congested areas. Seems obvious to me.

ReadTheSmallPrint

Lan Drober? More like Schizophrenic Droner... One
minute on the side of 4x4 driving Chelsea dwellers and
slagging off the 'sandalled underclass' (whatever that is),
and the next minute shining champion of the 'essential
worker' shafted by an unfair system. Sort your head out.
Reading between the lines I'd say that you're a 4x4
driving clone with a boring life and you lack the courage
to admit to yourself, let alone to your estate agent
friends, that you weren't fully able to stamp out your
social conscience. In short, you long for a pair of sandals.
I may be wrong about you, but I'm not wrong about
this: anyone who drives an SUV in London is a wanker.

From piss-take to serious debate, I don't think my abuse
of the 4x4/SUV is blinkered in any way, for what
possible justification can there be for owning or driving
such a vehicle in a city like London? Please answer that
without reference to wealth. The emissions they
produce are disproportionately and enormously high for
their vehicle size and class. They guzzle fuel with engine
sizes typically starting at 3500 cc. They take up more
parking space than reasonably sized cars and yes, my
sandal-wearing friends, they are more dangerous to
other road users and pedestrians in collisions because of
their great bulk and height. The shame of all this is that
SUVs are generally driven by intelligent people who
should know better.

Moving on, the argument about the economic effect
of the C-charge is an interesting one; however, any

business balanced so precariously as to have died with the introduction of the C-charge, I would argue, was not a viable, successful business in the first place, and as such should rightly go to the wall in the face of leaner competition.

As for 'essential workers', in the main they have never driven to work, because they don't have the money, they realise how wasteful it is and that the public transport system works within reason, wherever you live. I think that Lan Drober wouldn't know an essential worker if one of them smacked him/her in the face which, if he/she ever meets me, is exactly what will happen.

Billy the Bull

Sorry to prolong another raging LbL argument, but I'd just like to belatedly thank Lan Drober for his defence of 4x4 drivers. I'd always tended to believe in the popular stereotype of 4x4 drivers as blinkered, self-righteous, misguided snobs who genuinely think that owning a really really big car is some sort of status symbol, and probably use snotty terminology like 'sandalled under-class' and 'bleating have-nots' to describe people who are not similarly enamoured of really really big cars – who are clearly only jealous of the lucky 4x4 owners' wealth and status.

I'd just like to says thanks to Lan for confirming all my

favourite prejudices about 4x4 drivers! Billy the Bull, keep up the inflammatory posts...

Carty

What fun this 4x4 debate is. I can't wait for the next instalment. But that's only because I can't wait to see my name in print. Brilliant.

Name withheld for comic effect

ENTERTAINMENT, SERVICES AND SO ON

LONDON IS... THE CONTENTS OF THE Queen's purse and bare yooting in the streets; London is animals with personality disorders, depressed and broken people buying each other paintings and smokers and non-smokers living in near perfect harmony; London is choirs, pool halls, fitness enthusiasts and cabbage-growers; London is limescale and how to get rid of it...

Which period of London's history would you like to experience?

'I would have jumped into my time machine, maybe I would give Jack the Ripper a kiss and also the Kray twins and then I would have bought the whole of Shoreditch for a couple of pounds and kept it till today. Then I would jump back and sit in Hoxton Square today and smile about my wealth.'

 *Christina Skreiberg*, magazine editor

Personal

THERAPY

This is kind of personal, but I'm throwing it out there to the LbL community. Does anyone know of a good psychotherapist in south London? As we all know, living in this great city is not without its vicissitudes, and an, ahem, friend of mine recently suffered something of a 'derailment': he lost his job, his girlfriend and his self-confidence. Getting back on track has proved problematic, as even the simplest of tasks are complicated by paralysing anxiety, and procrastination brought on by a crisis of self-esteem. Does anyone know of someone in a similar situation who benefited from a particular therapist? These things are hard to talk about, even to friends, which makes it difficult to find people who have recovered from similar predicaments, and to discover who exactly it was that was able to help them turn things around.

Thierry Ennui

Your, ahem, 'friend' should ask their GP for a referral to a clinical psychologist. Therapy should be available on the NHS, and private therapy can be massively expensive I think. I was referred for cognitive behavioural therapy following a troubling spot of depression last year, the idea of CBT being to identify the negative thoughts as you have them and learning coping mechanisms to break the cycle that causes you to spiral into a hideous circle of self-doubt and low self-esteem that renders you unable to do much except stare at the ceiling. It may sound a bit wanky, but it's actually very practical, and just the very fact that you're taking action to address the problem can make you feel better.

You don't say where your friend is in south London, but I was registered with a GP in Foxley Square Surgery in SW9, who had a clinical psychologist attached. When I recently moved house, I phoned my new Primary Care Trust and asked which GPs had psychologists attached, and they put me in touch with a local Patient Advisory Liaison Service, who helped me register with a new GP that offered a psychology service onsite. GPs can vary in their responses to depression, and there's only so much you can get out of a seven-minute appointment, but if you go in and specifically ask for referral to a therapist they should help you.

Also, you might be surprised how sympathetic your friends can be. I've been making a real effort to tell people that I'm on anti-depressants, and whilst most have been pretty shocked (I have a good job, good social life, and usually come across as pretty upbeat, and am pretty happy most of the time apart from regular horrible depressive episodes) no one has reacted negatively. I'm not shouting it from the rooftops, but I'm starting to speak to close friends and family about it. Having said that, it's taken approximately six years to get that far, so I appreciate how hard it can be. Mostly, don't be too hard on yourself. You're seeking help and this will pass. Good luck.

Kate

Jenny Edwards in Beckenham (jenny@jennyedwards.biz) is very good and BACP registered. She helped me loads with some bereavement issues.

always delayed

WPF in Kensington (www.wpf.org.uk), who offer once-a-week counselling or more regular psychotherapy. They also offer a low-cost service, and if you don't want to travel to High Street Kensington they will be able to refer you to a therapist near you. They take the psychodynamic/psychoanalytic approach if that appeals to you. Alternatively a good place to start would be the BACP website: www.bacp.co.uk/seeking_therapist/index.html.

tootgirl

BREAK UP

I just broke up with my partner today. What do you do to shake the break-up blues? (And I don't want to jump into another relationship!) You know, pigtails and skipping down the road happiness that we all need when feeling blue...

Pigtails-girl

Drink Tequila and sleep with random strangers.

What else?

Random Stranger

As one who has been there, my suggestion would be to do all the things that you wouldn't have been able to do in your previous relationship. Forgive me for sounding patronising but just go out and enjoy what London has to offer, reacquaint yourself with your old friends (there are always people you stop seeing when you're with someone), take up those offers that previously you may have turned down. Failing that, just go for a long walk – I always find the view from the South Bank or the top of Greenwich Park so uplifting. Good luck.

Cravatekid

It's about getting your perspective back – I suggest you get some headphones (and they don't have to be white), put your favourite and most familiar music on, and take a long walk around London at night. Start at *Buckingham Palace*, walk down Pall Mall and then to the *Houses of Parliament*. Cross the river and watch the moonlight dance on the water. Sit on a bench on the South Bank. Walk along it, as far as *St Paul's*. The solidity of the London skyline can be amazingly comforting, as well as the sight of people walking, walking, walking. You have no idea who they are and what their stories are, but they are there in the London night with you. All of this combines to give you the feeling of the world moving on, how much there is in it and your space in the mix.

I hope you feel better soon.

feelinghappy

Pigtails-girl, London is the best partner you can ever have. It constantly surprises, keeps you warm and safe, makes you smile, and cheekily takes money out of your purse occasionally. And it doesn't laugh at your clothes.

Mamfer (in comfy trousers watching 'Titanic')

HYPNO — CLAUSTROPHOBIA

My girlfriend, being mad, refuses to travel on trains, planes or – especially – tubes, because she becomes claustrophobic and has panic attacks. Has anyone else overcome something like this, and if so, how? I'm thinking hypnotherapy would be the laziest solution...

Bobby

I suffer from panic attacks and anxiety, have an incredible fear of flying and absolutely hate needles. I don't like going on tubes and get off if I feel anxious or if it's too full. I don't suffer from claustrophobia as such, but I'm imagining that a panic attack on a tube or confined space is pretty similar! Hypnotherapy will definitely work – it helped me loads. It's very expensive though, and something she would need a few sessions of, but well worth it. Have a look at www.thehypnotherapyassociation.co.uk – anxiety and panic attacks are not pleasant so anything is worth a go!

cinap

Tubes are the foul subterranean entrails of the London beast, stuffed with the day's foetid offerings. Having said that, I find that Bach's Rescue Remedy can keep me on

an even keel. I don't believe in all that alternative
medicine stuff, so I suppose it's the placebo effect.

Tokugawa

I can recommend a brilliant hypnotherapist who is a
friend of mine but none the less has treated a lot of
people with all manner of phobias from flying to toilet-
related incidents – all cured in about three sessions by
hypnotherapy. Her name is Jessica Robinson and her
website is at www.jessicarobinson.co.uk.

heppy

SELF-IMPROVEMENT

SMOKERS

**I am desperate to give up the old death sticks and
have been thinking about getting hypnotised as a last
resort. However, being an LbLer I am deeply cynical
and can't help thinking that I will be conned out of
loads of cash and still be gasping for my Silk Cuts.
Any advice, recommendations, stories?**

fagashlil

I'm in the process of successfully giving up (as in, I've not cheated so far and don't think I'm going to but it's only been a few weeks!) thanks to the much-advertised NHS stop smoking people. I am going to a Smoking Cessation Clinic, which is much more fun than it sounds, at the Royal London and highly recommend it!

Little G

Easy Stop is a franchise with practitioners across London: www.easystop.co.uk/consultants/london.htm.

I saw Andy Wilkinson at the Clapham Common clinic for two sessions, a week apart. The process was easy and surprisingly pleasurable. It cost £175 and the price may have gone up since then, but it was the best money I've ever spent and they give a lifetime guarantee!

nosmoking

Oh fagashlil, I despair of ever giving up the evil weed. I have tried hypnotherapy and I have to say I think it was all a load of old bunk. I went there quite open-minded mind you, willing to give myself up to the mystical lady who could cure me of my nasty, stinky habit. I WANTED to stop. Anyway, two hours later and £200 lighter she assured me I wouldn't want to smoke again. I was cured. I was a NON-SMOKER. The lying bitch. I asked why I couldn't remember anything she'd said to me after the first five minutes and she said it was because I was in a deep hypnotic trance. I say it was because I WAS COCKING WELL ASLEEP YOU DAFT BINT! Needless to say four hours after that I was ready to kill for a fag, had a massive row with the bf, stormed out of the house and bought a pack of 20. I'm down to five per day now. Unless there's booze involved obviously. Good luck though, it might work for you!

always delayed

Allen Carr works wonders. I read most of (I didn't finish it!) the seemingly endless *The Only Way to Stop Smoking Permanently*, put out a half-finished fag over five years ago and haven't touched one since – no cold turkey, no withdrawal, no willpower needed. I think the reasoning behind it is that if you can put up with his writing style then stopping smoking is a doddle in comparison. He's got a clinic in Raynes Park as well if the books don't work. It's a bit pricier though.

iSleepDiagonal

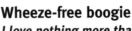

Wheeze-free boogie
I love nothing more than casting off the working week with a good dance to indie, '60s and alternative mixes. Problem is I really don't like spending all night choking on cigarette smoke and waking up the next morning stinking of fags and wheezing like I've got a 40-a-day habit. I was wondering whether any of you fine Londoners could recommend any decent alternative venues which are either well-ventilated or ideally, actually smoke-free? Thanks for any tips – I'll be the cute one bouncing up and down on the dance floor without a care in the world until the early hours of the morning.

Daisychain

Oh FFS!!! Look, if the politicians have it their way they'll all be bloody smoke-free in a couple of years, so until then shut up and let us enjoy clubbing and smoking together. Dublin's only a couple of quid return with Ryanair, try there in the meantime. It's only an hour away and will cost you not much more than a taxi to Brixton.

Tris2000

CREATIVE FULFILMENT

Having made some major life changes, I'm now trying to work out what I want to do with my newfound 'work–life balance'. I feel like I've been starving my creative side, so I'd like to do something musicy, arty or to do with writing. I enjoy singing and writing but have no artistic talent as far as I know. I'm poor, so it needs to be something ultra cheap. Anyone have any suggestions? Maybe some people who like to get together and make some music and wouldn't mind an extra (very nice!) girl to come along and join in?! I'm going to get back into exploring galleries and things, but any particular suggestions would be most welcome! Cheers!

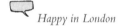

Happy in London

What you want is a book called *The Artists Way* by Julia Cameron – it's bloody brilliant to get your creative juices flowing, it's a 12-week course which transforms anyone into a fulfilled, arty, creative and entirely wonderful person. It's brilliant. You get lots of activities to do each week, and ideas for how to convert your interests into creative activities, and how to revive things you did when you were six that you've probably completely forgotten about. If you buy from Amazon, click through from the Burma campaign link to give them a donation too: www.burmacampaign.org.uk/ merchandise.html.

EmmaN1

I'm involved in running a Brazilian drumming workshop in Stockwell; it costs £5 to bang drums from 7:30–10 p.m. every Thursday (all instruments are provided). Very creative, very exciting, and we cater for all skills from novice to mestre! To find out more visit: www.maracatu.co.uk/

Hope to see you there!

Oli #2

I have just the answer for you. I have recently started teaching myself the ukulele and have been having a terrific time doing so. They are cheap (£10–20 off eBay), very easy to play and there are lessons on the Internet so you don't need proper lessons. I'm not particularly musical either but I've found it really addictive. You get yourself one of them and you can come and join in with me and my housemates anytime!

Banana Girl aka the ukulady

BIKRAM WITHOUT THE STENCH

Non-crusty yoga – does such a thing exist? Does anyone know of somewhere in London where I could do Bikram Yoga (the sort you do in a really hot room) in a really modern, hygienic environment? I have tried the new Bikram Yoga centres in West London (Fulham/Chiswick) but they are a bit alternative/vegan for me, with lots of crusty people who look and smell like they don't believe in modern Western grooming products/practices… good for them I say, but I'm a bit of a princess and it's just not my scene. Also, all the classes are mixed and they don't make men wear shirts. If I want to be surrounded by sweaty half-naked men I can go to *GAY* where at least the guys are hot-looking! Basically, I love the way Bikram Yoga makes me feel but I really hate being surrounded by loads of smelly, hairy, crusty people while I do it. I need some kind of slick, modern, Holmes Place-style Bikram Yoga centre, ideally offering women-only classes… Does such a place exist? Where does Madonna go? I've tried *Triyoga*, but they don't do Bikram.

Inflexible princess

Answer to the Yoga Chick from my colleague who is a hardcore Bikram Yoga chap... 'Only official Bikram studios which have been through the training process in LA with Mr Bikram himself can offer Bikram so you're not going to get a Holmes place vibe... Her best option is to go to *Bikram North* (Kentish Town) www.bikramyoga.co.uk – it's been renovated quite recently and it's a big studio and go to a daytime or morning session in the week... always less busy and more females than male. They encourage men to wear shorts only cos it's so bleeding hot and it doesn't restrict movement. If you practise yoga, expect people stripped down... that's the way it's done. If you can't stand the heat get out the bleeding kitchen. So in short, sweaty yoga means sweaty place to do it in. Am not thinking about men in small shorts doing sweaty yoga now I promise!

Bezmina

There was always Bikram Yoga advertised as I waited for my bus on Provost Street, N1 (Old Street). A quick Google search reveals its location on Vestry Street (round the corner), and a link to other locations in Queens Park and Chalk Farm. I don't partake myself, but friends attended other classes/gym on Vestry street and I don't recall being regaled with any yarns about crusty vegan types.

www.bikramyoga.co.uk/intro.html.

Inflexible and staying that way

MASSAGE

Can anyone recommend somewhere to get a good massage from nice people in pleasant surroundings? Anywhere in London will do, and I'm not after a particular type: Indian head, full body, foot tickle – I don't mind really. I've never been before and don't really know where to start.

Stressed Eric

Check out this website for Indian Head Massage in central and south west London or in the comfort of your own home: www.treatmindbodysole.com. The lady who runs this is very nice indeed.

PS. She is my mum.

The Sinsinsanity Kid

I can wholeheartedly recommend Jon Gee who has magic fingers and will get straight to the cause of your pain – you will leave walking on air! He once massaged my hips – a new one on me, but worked a treat. Check out www.angelmassagetherapy.com.

pockettiger

The Mary Ward Centre runs weekend massage courses which are really cheap. It's a full-day course for a number of Saturdays – and of course half the time you're practising the techniques and the other half you're being massaged. It's a great way to get a free massage and it's a skill that makes you very popular!

Masseuse

I am a fully qualified Holistic Massage and Thai Yoga Massage Practitioner and Baby Massage Instructor. I offer my therapies in south west London both through home visits and local treatment rooms. I specialise in prenatal and postnatal massage and support but also work with clients of all ages and abilities. If you are interested in learning more about my therapies please get in touch and I will be happy to answer your questions. Email me info@marieortutherapies.co.uk or check out my website at www.marieortutherapies.co.uk.

Marie Ortu Therapies

I use Ego Spa just outside Greenwich. The girl working there gives an excellent full body massage – the best I have ever had. It normally costs about £35 for an hour. Their phone number is 020 8293 1901. I used to go there when I lived in Greenwich, and now that I live in Waterloo, it is well worth the trip.

Henry

I work in a place called *Cucumba* in Poland Street, W1.
Does great massage – on a chair or on a couch –
including sports and deep tissue, and we'll even make
you a cup of tea and play you something nice (I find a bit
of Nick Drake or the occasional Chet Baker goes down
well)

jarwobble

SPORTS AND HOBBIES

BALLS ETC.

**Does anyone know of anywhere in norf London
where I can get a friendly game of basketball? Just
want to shoot some hoops with a like-minded bunch
of people doing it for fun.**

Kendall Festruss

I've never played but always wanted to. Trouble is the
only teams I found already know everything and are
really intimidating when you try to learn – yes of course
I'm going to drop the ball and miss the net, so why shout
at me? So does anyone know of somewhere a complete
beginner could go in south/west London – I live in
Tooting and work in South Ken. I just love sports and

every couple of years I like to try a new one; this way some sports I carry on for years like cycling and diving and others, well they just disappear.

sportforgirls

I run a sport/adventure club called 8th Day UK, which is aimed at people in exactly the same boat as you. We organise loads of different sports and activities for our members both in the evenings during the week and at weekends and even some holidays. These range from just meeting up for running or for games in the park on a sunny evening (like touch rugby, rounders, volleyball etc.) to one-off lessons in things like poledancing, fencing or kickboxing, for example. We also try and get groups together to play random stuff for a laugh, and have so far done broomball (ice hockey but without ice skates and with a broom and a ball!), underwater ice hockey (brilliant!) and are soon to stage what I think might be the UK's first proper dodgeball game (just got the balls from the USA!!). It's all about just trying new stuff with a bunch of other people who are all up for having a bit of a laugh. We also do stuff like karting, surf weekends, stunt riding (on horses, beginners welcome!!), skiing holidays, paintball... and anything else we can think of!! Check us out at www.8thdayuk.com – we're all really friendly and you can come to one our of socials or any one event before

joining to see what you think. Hope to see you at
something soon!

Ross

I have just started playing basketball in Wimbledon
with *PlayFit* (www.playfit.co.uk). Essentially, this is a
sports club for those that prefer the social side of sport as
much playing the game itself. Sports on offer range
from netball to volleyball and, lucky for you, basketball.
They run various sessions as well as lots of social events.
Sessions are based on ability as opposed to gender,
which in my eyes is no bad thing! Highly recommended. Cheers.

Cookie

ALLOTMENT

**Dear London, my Hackney-based missus has been
struggling for years to get an allotment to snatch a
bit of the good life locally. She's been on the local
allotment society's list for over three years, but still
has no idea of where she stands in the pecking order
for plots. Apparently local councils have a duty to
provide each of us with a plot of land to grow our
dinner (probably ancient compensation for nicking
our common land). Can anyone shed any light on**

this? And has anyone successfully enforced this right?

Dave

From what I understand, you can sign up for an allotment in any borough: some have shortages and some have surpluses. So if you live in Hackney and nothing's doing you might check out Tower Hamlets etc. Right about now's the time people get kicked off for not keeping them up, so you may be in with a chance. Having just got one (in LB Ealing), I know it also helps to know a mason.

Green Bum

As I understand it, local councils are theoretically obliged to provide allotments roughly to the level that there is demand for them, but in practice this doesn't really get enforced (as witness the 3–4+ year waiting lists in many parts of London). Indeed, a lot of councils are trying to get rid of allotments rather than providing more (so they can sell the land off to developers to build yet more posh-yet-teeny flats on). Might be worth her contacting her local councillor about it if she feels like kicking up a fuss about the provision. Also, has she tried phoning the allotment society (or going down the allotments on a Saturday to have a chat with folk) to see how the waiting list is doing? My local society (in Bermondsey) were very

informative when I was on the waiting list (I finally got
my allotment in September, hurrah!). And tell her, when
she does get an allotment, she should invest in a storm
kettle: www.eydonkettle.co.uk. Boil water for your
cuppa in a couple of minutes, then sit in the corner of the
allotment surveying your domain... best feeling ever, and
the tea tastes great!

Juliet

WINE AND POOL

**Happy New Year. I have two New Year's resolutions
that I would like people's help with: (a) a decent,
down-to-earth wine course that isn't up its own
jaxxi with all this 'ooh, I'm getting guava, I'm
getting gerbils, I'm getting tarmac' nonsense; (b) is
there anywhere in London that actually gives classes
in how to play pool? I've never got round to it, and
now when I go to the pub I have to make excuses
otherwise I'm just pathetic. It's one of these games
that, magically, you're just supposed to know how
to play but, er, I don't. Yeah, I know I could battle
on with mates, but I'd like to learn so the next time
I'm with friends I can stride up to the table with
confidence! Thanks.**

2006already?

I can really recommend going to the tastings which are held periodically in a wine shop called (rather dramatically) the *Theatre of Wine* in Greenwich. They focus on a region or country and about 10–15 people of all ages and backgrounds go. Some are a bit pompous but loads of people know nothing (like me) and have a good time tasting the wine and eating the meat and cheese which are provided too. I find this a good way to dabble in wine tasting without signing up for a formal course: www.theatreofwine.com. Generally, it is also a brilliant shop.

Emma

I can't help with the wine tasting course unfortunately (my palate isn't advanced enough – I'm always 'getting' vinegar), but for pool tuition there's a few things you can do. I presume you were talking about 'English' pool (on the small tables in most pubs), but if you get to grips with any cue sport (e.g. American pool, snooker), you should find the small table a doddle. If you head down to the *Riley's American Pool and Snooker Hall* in Semley Place near *Victoria Coach Station*, you should be able to get lessons in (American) pool or snooker from Rico Diks – a former European champion, and just about the nicest guy I've ever met. He's helped me become fairly handy at American pool (which is actually a lot more fun than English pool when you get

into it) – and it all translates nicely to the small tables
you find in pubs.

mrpies

The *London Wine Academy* (Google it) does a couple of
six-week courses which are pretty good. I was given one
for Christmas last year. Not full of wine snobs, just down-
to-earth people who generally want to get a bit more
knowledge to navigate their way around a wine list
confidently. I can't guarantee you won't be getting
'gooseberry, nutmeg and damp dog overtones' out of a
glass of plonk by the end, but that's half the fun.

edmundG

GYM

**It's that time of year again; looking for a decent
gym. Can someone recommend a decent gym
in the middle of town, or Holborn/King's Cross/
Islington/Highbury way. I don't mind spending
good money on one that's spacious, with good
facilities (especially free-weights), opens early and
doesn't have pathetic hours at weekends, and has a
decent lounge area to chill out in afterwards. What
really gets bonus points from me is good staff who
are friendly, proactive, and come forward to offer**

help and advice rather than just standing there laughing among themselves but look at the punters as if they are an inconvenience, counting down the minutes till their shift ends (well, that was my impression of *Virgin Active Islington*, anyway). Thanks in advance for your suggestions.

Whwhwh05

I went through a similar thing last year, and searched every gym I could find around Islington (where I live) and Westminster (where I work). I ended up at *Fitness First*. The one at Islington is a premier club, but worth joining. Let me just say the staff are fantastic. I was assaulted at work in June and went through a really difficult time. I went to the gym and the staff gave me a cheap manicure, some free sessions with a personal trainer, a free sun-bed session, and they started phoning me to check how I was. I'm telling you these guys are fantastic. The place is clean, there's never a queue for a treadmill, free drinks and papers, DVD rental, sauna, sun-bed, aromatherapy room... The only downside (which isn't the end of the world but my personal gripe) is that they no longer offer shampoo and conditioner free! But hey, can't have everything. And when you join you can use any *Fitness First* gym.

bettyvirago

CHOIR

Once upon a time (in Sydney) I used to sing in a great choir. No auditions were required but it was still large enough and good enough to warrant singing in. I have looked into re-joining a choir here in London, but I have noticed that most of the 'good ones' demand an audition. I can sing but I am too shy to audition – which explains why I want to sing in a choir rather than, say, on *Pop Idol*. Does anyone know of a great choir in or around central London that will not force me to audition?

the mousegirl

The choir I sing in may be up your street and I realised that I stupidly did not include the name of my choir or the website in my post the other week. We are 'Chantage' and can be found online at www.chantage.org. We don't have a formal audition process so look under 'about us' and then 'joining chantage' and you'll get the full details. Happy singing!

Choir girl with a dark side

Try Islington Choral Society. They are a good quality choir, with a social feel and regular concerts. They meet on Tuesdays at 7.30 p.m.

Have fun.

Baberuth

MISCELLANY

PSYCHIC

I am looking for a genuine (and non-exorbitant) psychic or tarot reader. Have any of my fellow-Londoners been to one who was spookily accurate? And not just about the past (because I think talking about the past is more of face reading than genuine psychic powers) but also about the future. A friend and I want to go to one just for a laugh, but want it to be someone who has been tried and tested. Thanks!

rt5mrt

Good question! Your man is Allan Reinhardt – absolutely fantastic psychic and tarot reader – totally genuine. Be open-minded though – he's really bloody good and if you think it's just a laugh you might get a shock at how accurate he is. Very down to earth, nice bloke. He'll give you a tape recording of your reading to take away with you. He's based out west but it's worth the trek – either at Motherearth, 205 Acton Lane, London, W4 5DA. Tel: 020 8354 2248 or at the Holistic Centre, 5 Devonshire Road W4 2EU Tel: 020 8987 0364. www.theholisticcentre.co.uk. Good luck!

EmmaN1

I went to see a psychic counsellor who is amazing. Did past present and future but also talked about how that could positively affect my life... I was a sceptic until it all came true this year (went to see her about six months ago) – she is really friendly too! www.lightofspirit.co.uk.

ladypenelope

Whistling while they work

In the hope that the people who sit behind me at work receive the LbL email, could I ask them to stop fucking whistling? It's driving me to the edge of insanity. Do it in your spare time or, at the very least, out of earshot of someone who is planning to throttle you fairly soon. Otherwise, you are very pleasant people. Ta.

Conan Hairspray

PET PSYCHOLOGIST

I appreciate that this might mark me out as a loony, but have any readers ever employed the services of a pet psychologist? My cat is going mental in the night and I am becoming increasingly desperate. Does it work or is it a big ol' waste of money?

Miss Margo

Pet psychologists DO work – for dogs anyway. We had a terrible time with an RSPCA dog that had a mega case of separation anxiety. Barkbusters sorted him in one session!! www.barkbusters.co.uk.

patzee

Loony, for your mad kitty you may want to try the cat psychologist Vicky Halls who is based in Kent. She is not only recommended by our very good vet but has written a humorous yet very useful book on cat psychology called *Cat Confidential – The Book Your Cat Would Like You to Read*. The book was so good that I didn't need to employ her services after all, I just did what it said in the book and saw no more of the said cat problem! Finally, reading it was a real eye-opener even for someone who considers themselves a rather experienced cat-owner.

Kat

It's worth speaking to a vet who specialises in behaviour problems. Unfortunately, it's not always cheap, especially as to really work out what the cat is reacting to might involve a home visit. But it's probably worth it to get the problem sorted. It's usually a case of working out exactly what is triggering the cat's behaviour and then trying to prevent or reduce it. Sometimes drug therapies are useful in the short term, which is why it's better seeing a specialist vet rather than a non-veterinary behaviourist. Additionally, a vet will be able to determine if it is definitely a behaviour problem and that there is not an underlying medical problem (certain conditions, such as thyroid disease, can cause behavioural changes in cats). You're probably best speaking to your usual vet first and arranging a referral if necessary. Hope that helps.

C Fi

Give it carrots and taurine. I believe that cats do not have a psyche therefore any psychological treatment would have no affect on the cat.

Dr Lake

Facial
Does anyone know where I could find a beauty salon in London, preferably West End area but not essential, other than the London School of Beauty *in Charlotte Street, that offers what's called a 'high frequency' facial. I've Googled, I've phoned, and I've even popped into a couple, but nothing. Thanks for the info if you have any.*

in-need-of-a-facial

Try the London School of Beauty and Make-up *in Charlotte Street. Apparently they do it. Their website is: www.lond-est.com/Salon.htm.*

britbird

A 'high frequency' facial'?!? Isn't that sometimes known as Bukkake? And the Japanese use it in reference to noodles. Weird.

Juvey

SPIT AND POLISH

My second least favourite chore is polishing shoes. That paint-type stuff is grotesque, those little tubs of Kiwi are the work of the devil, and brushes fester darkly under the stairs. The only shoe shiner I know sits in the Burlington Arcade, but even I balk at paying eight quid congestion, another two for parking, and three more for an (albeit splendid) spit and polish. Does anyone know of somebody in NW London? Or better still, a business that'll do 'em in bulk?

Fred Titmus

If you are looking for shoeshine boys why not try *Streetshine*. It's a company that takes on homeless people and fits them out with the kit to shine shoes, then they go round big companies and effectively become self-employed. Helps them get back on the social ladder etc.: www.streetshine.com.

The Assassin Prince

Hey FredTitmus, I'm curious to know what your least favourite chore is? Mine used to be ironing until I made the executive decision to just leave my suit jacket on all day thus negating the need iron anymore. In fact, I don't own an iron anymore.

Bored

AN ORIGINAL GIFT

It's around that time of year when the usual conundrum hits me. Just what am I going to buy my other half for her birthday? It gets more and more difficult as each year passes and I'm narrowly in danger or becoming my father and purchasing a nice blender from *QVC*. After occasionally traipsing the streets of London for something original and getting nowhere – but rather flustered – fast, I wondered if anyone knew of any websites or shops where I'd be able to buy something that wouldn't be considered 'the usual'? In fact, just any good gift websites that don't try and sell me every gift under the sun draped in leather with her initials gold-embossed in the corner. I've seemingly exhausted every unconventional (yet somewhat predictable) gift known to man. She's jumped out of the plane. She's got a newspaper from the day that she was born. She's done the spa day. Hell, I've even personalised her teacup! Help me LbLers. You're my only hope.

Jeff Camp

How about a nice weekend in Bruges staying in a castle: http://tinyurl.com/pca2t. I was taken here by my girlfriend for a birthday and can recommend it. Plus

Bruges is well known for its chocolates and beer (find *The Bruges Bear* for the best choice). Of course, if you're feeling extravagant there is always Antwerp's diamond market down the road...

Stiltskin

One of the best presents I've ever received was a globe which proudly resides on my desk. It's one of the old-fashioned sepia-toned ones. I guess this is only good if she likes that kind of thing, but being fond of travel myself and working in the travel industry, it was perfect! Try www.justglobes.co.uk. Another great present was a first edition of a book I love, so that might be an option? Or take her to Brighton for the weekend. I love Brighton!!

The girl who has everything

Always a thorny one! Not really sure of a site other than the usual suspects – www.lastminute.com – tickets for a show, opera, restaurant, citybreak, Tiffany, silly pressies on Firebox etc., but dependent on budget, why not go to the RA's summer exhibition and buy a painting (not necessarily too pricey) and then take her there on her birthday for a day out and show her your present. In a similar vein, sponsor her favourite animal at the zoo in her name (wildly varying costs) and take her to visit the penguin/tiger/chinchilla in question. If you and her friends have time on your hands, then you can organise a treasure hunt around London – each destination you meet a different friend holding the next clue (and a bottle and glasses), and you collect everyone and end up at favourite restaurant for a big birthday meal and at end of the meal, final clue to your present whatever 'ordinary' gift you may choose to buy her. Top end of the King's Road is pretty good for boutiques with different furniture/clothes/jewellery (but pricey). Oh, and a final thought, what about the table in the kitchen at Ramsay's? Alternatively, Diamonique is a girl's best friend...

Citybumpkin

Have a look through the *Daily Candy* archives. They advertise (although I don't think they call it that) unusual stuff and are usually good for a present – www.dailycandy.co.uk.

shopaholic

Well done, Jeff Camp. You do seem to put in a lot of effort there – with which I sympathise, being someone who gets very distressed before every special date. Mainly because my boyfriend couldn't be more difficult to please... but I digress. Have you had a look at www.boysstuff.co.uk? They used to have a 'girlsstuff' domain as well, but now everything is concentrated on this website. Check the 'Stuff 4 Girls' section. Mostly you'll find silly little presents (the useless colourful things are my favourites), but then you could maybe mix it with a more conventional present? Good luck there.

Senhorita

Something for the missus eh? Try www.iwantoneofthose.com. Loads of ideas and nonsense gifts that you can use after she's finished with you.

spazwit

Oh I know the perfect place for you. Try www.goodgifts.org – they're brilliant. All the gifts are really ethical as well... you can pay for anything really, from a camel to an acre of rainforest... check out their catalogue, there are over a hundred unusual gifts. They're extremely reputable (been going for 25 years). A work colleague got a 'supergoat' from them last year and is very happy. Also see this – http://ethicalgifts.blogspot.com/ – if you're also considering something unusual for Father's Day.

Mestalla

Jeff, I too have trouble finding interesting gifts, but over the past year or so I've found some interesting things online. Try *Etsy* (www.etsy.com) or *Atypyk* (www.atypyk-e-shop.com) for some fairly unique stuff. Also, *Nudo* (www.nudo-italia.com) is a brilliant gift – adopt an olive tree! – which I can say from experience is definitely well received. Perhaps not suitable for this occasion (too small), but also worth mentioning is *Dough Dough* (www.doughdough.com), a UK site which sends muffins, brownies and so forth in the post – I've sent about a dozen and they always arrive on time and the recipients are always pleasantly surprised. Finally, I've collected 30 or so other gift-related links which you'll find on my shared Delicious bookmarks, if the above isn't enough: http://del.icio.us/paulfarnell/presents. Hope that helps!

Salted

Get her a portable vintage record player (eBay?), and a stack of old records you know she'll love... that would be my favourite present. Or a course in something you know she's interested in...

Pooka

A chocolate fountain... I got one from my boyfriend, and although I was nagging to him and most others around me for one I still didn't expect one... just make sure you get chocolate to go with it! Useless if your girlfriend is on a diet.

Nerys

PAINTINGS

I wondered if anyone could tell me where to go if I wanted to buy a painting (or just generally, some art) in London? I thought it would be a really nice gift for a friend of mine but I have no idea how to go about looking for something suitable. Unfortunately, I'm a bit restricted budget-wise, but am just looking for something small so it won't take over her room. I'm thinking £150 at most. Is that unrealistic? I've honestly no idea. I'd love to hear some suggestions! Thanks.

Bobble

My boyfriend recently bought me a piece of art for my thirtieth birthday from www.castlegalleries.co.uk in Bluewater, although they have various branches around the country. It's not quite London, but close enough. They had an amazing selection of gorgeous paintings, prints and sculptures, and although they were not cheap I am sure you could find something within your budget, or if not then at least some advice. They were not at all snooty either. By the way, a piece of art is a great present for a special birthday, in case anyone needs gift ideas.

TK

I used to buy the odd cheapish painting or print from a firm called *Abbott and Holder*. They used to be down in Barnes but are now in Museum Street by the *British Museum*. Prices have gone up but I see from their website, for example, a nineteenth-century watercolour of a rambling watermill by William Linton for 95 quid. It might be worth a look.

andyb

Have you been to *Bankside Gallery* – www.banksidegallery.com – on the river front next to *Tate Modern*? They sell very affordable prints and paintings. I've bought from there before and they're really friendly.

Hanger

You could probably do worse than popping down to the *London Open Air Gallery* which is run on the Bayswater Road on a Sunday morning. Something for everyone I think (just as a cheeky plug, my mate Steve exhibits down there and on www.pop-portraits.com).

Naeonlite

THE QUEEN'S PURSE

Does anyone know what the Queen puts in her purse? I can't imagine what she would have in there.

Curious

Hey Curious, if you'd watched the highlights of the Queen's eightieth birthday church service, you'd have seen her open her purse!! And she has money in it! With her face on!!! How weird is that? She also appeared to have a vibrator and a pair of love eggs but I have to admit, my eyes aren't what they were.

Juvey

YOOTING

The *Islington Bar* was raided and shut down by the police a few weeks ago, bare yooting outside all the time so good riddance too. *Lincoln Lounge* (York Way) is a top place though, definitely recommended.

Salem

Do I need to get out more? What in the name of all that is holy is bare yooting?

Griff

'Yooting' is a deep plasma etching technique used to produce high–aspect ratio polymer microstructures. 'Bare', I am told, means 'a lot of, very'. So it sounds like there was a lot of unwelcome bioengineering going on outside the *Islington Bar*.

Frank Muir

Surely that's a BLUFF.

Alan Coren

Money-saving ideas
Christmas is coming up and for some unknown reason a hole in my pocket has meant that my finances won't stretch to gorgeous expensive presents. As such I will be making as many of them as I possibly can... Now I know that Christmas is far away and I too hate the fact that the shops start pushing Christmas far too early, but this bid to save money will not save me time. Therefore I have to start making them now. Please give me your suggestions.

bablet

Blow out an egg, write a loving message on a small piece of paper, insert the paper into the hole and let loved ones crack them open on Christmas Day. Personal, interactive and all for the cost of, well... an egg. Like a fortune cookie but without the cookie or fortune bit and, if you're writing a love poem, will probably make less sense than a Chinese proverb. If your finances are really stretched, you could also use the egg contents within your baking recipes. Make all cheques payable to...

Scouse_Boy

Dude – are you mental? My girl would freak if I gave her one of these.

shockedatfreakyeggthing

KETTLESCUM

Does anyone know what that horrid flaky stuff floating around in my kettle is, and more importantly, how to get rid of it? I thought it might

be normal limescale/kettle fur, except every other time I've seen that it's lighter in colour and looks more like a mineral deposit (which is essentially what it is). This stuff's just crunchy flaky stuff that sticks to the element and the sides of the kettle, or floats around in the water. I thought there might be more to it than limescale perhaps due to some idiosyncrasy of London's water supply?

mrfrisky

If you leave a teaspoon inside your kettle, the scum will stick to the spoon instead of to the kettle, or the element, or floating around in the water. The spoon makes a bit of a rattle when the kettle boils sometimes, but it won't do any damage!

emmaN1

I was mildly interested in the kettlescum solutions as mine is a bit gammy but it doesn't bother me enough to remember to Google it. There is a lot of debate about transport and other things which is also interesting but a lighthearted break from it all is welcome.

Emma

Does anyone remember that programme on TV in which you could see Johnny Ball hang a lit candle from a length of plaited spaghetti?

boho

So, does anyone want to hear how I got on descaling my kettle?

mrfrisky

I do I do I do...! Love this site, and miss London.

exLondoner living way down SW

London by London by London
www.flickr.com/groups/LbL/pool/show

LbL

And Finally...

Before we go, we'd just like to thank everyone featured in this book for their contributions and for making the LbL community what it is today.

Thank you.

We'll leave you with a few more of our favourite quotes from some of our interviewees this year.

– LbL

What do you do to relax in London?
'Go for a walk in one of the many green spaces. Or watch a film at a cinema like the Curzon in Soho. Or have rampant sex by my window with the curtains open. Not necessarily in that order.'

 *Girl With a One-Track Mind, writer, sexpert*

What's the most irritating thing about London?
'It is driven by money so fiercely that the more substantial matters of life (i.e. love, spirit, art, humanity) are all trampled underfoot. Thus the

obedient corporate underling with an IKEA fit-out and an empty heart is king in this town. The rest of us get chased out of our houses, hang-outs, neighbourhoods, so that this creature can put his feet up to watch *Big Brother* and smugly contemplate his neatly planned future.'

Martin Craft, singer-songwriter

What's your most memorable tube experience?
'Isn't everyday an adventure? I'm guessing that the woman who started clipping her toenails while sitting next to me was pretty memorable. Or using my "detect-a-vom" superpower to neatly sidestep someone vomiting over my shoes on a couple of occasions. I guess I'll always remember getting excited about going to a "one under" (obviously in my ambulance role) only to find him sitting on the platform bench. I was exceedingly disappointed – does that make me a bad person?'

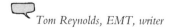
Tom Reynolds, EMT, writer

What's the most invigorating thing about London?

'Coming from a small town it's ace to see people dress however they like without fear of public humiliation or a beating. Saying that though, a bit of restraint would be nice occasionally. Yes I'm talking to you, Hoxton. I mean the return of the ironic moustache. What's going on there? What next? The Mullet? Eh? Oh.'

Andrew Laidlow, musician, Lucky Star

Which period of London's history would you like to experience?

'The 1960s – from 1965 to the end of 1969. I was in Her Majesty's Prison so I missed all the fun and sensuality of the great uprising I had helped to instigate. I still figure the Queen owes me at least one thousand orgasms.'

Brian Barrett, writer, free-thinker

FRIDAYCITIES: LONDON

Since the publication of the last book, London by London has changed dramatically. No longer merely a weekly email and accompanying annual, LbL has matured into a whole new virtual world, designed specifically to make your real life more enjoyable and fulfilling. www.fridaycities.com has taken the best aspects of the London by London community and blended them with the latest online technology to produce a website where you can share your wealth of London knowledge, have your London queries answered within 24 hours, meet a whole host of new and interesting people and find something to do when you've logged out and left your desk behind.

So if you're not already a member, what are you waiting for? Pop along to www.fridaycities.com and find out how you can become involved.

Join the community.

Share the knowledge.

Change your life.

Fridaycities. Join us.
http://london.fridaycities.com/signup
J8f7gy2xu

INDEX